SUMMER IN TOURAINE

The name Touraine is now a general word referring to the indefinite part of central France celebrated for its historical houses
and natural beauty. The author's aim in this enchanting work is
to provide the traveller, armchair and actual, with sufficient
intellectual equipment so that he may find the beautiful
châteaux of this region something more than coy lamentations
in stone and mortar. In this book the châteaux are explored in
connection with the times through which they have lived and
the people who have occupied them.

www.keganpaul.com

THE KEGAN PAUL
TRAVELLERS SERIES

THE CHÂTEAU OF LUYNES

A SUMMER IN
TOURAINE

The Indre et Loire of France

FREDERIC LEES

KEGAN PAUL

London • New York • Bahrain

First published in 2004 by
Kegan Paul Limited
UK: P.O. Box 256, London WC1B 3SW, England
Tel: 020 7580 5511 Fax: 020 7436 0899
E-Mail: books@keganpaul.com
Internet: http://www.keganpaul.com
USA: 61 West 62nd Street, New York, NY 10023
Tel: (212) 459 0600 Fax: (212) 459 3678
Internet: http://www.columbia.edu/cu/cup

Distributed by:
Turpin Distribution
Blackhorse Road
Letchworth, Herts. SG6 1HN
England
Tel: (01462) 672555 Fax: (01462) 480947
Email: books@turpinltd.com

Columbia University Press
61 West 62nd Street, New York, NY 10023
Tel: (212) 459 0600 Fax: (212) 459 3678
Internet: http://www.columbia.edu/cu/cup

ISBN: 0-7103-0889-2

British Library Cataloguing in Publication Data
A summer in the Touraine : the Indre et Loire of France. – New ed. – (Travellers series)
1.Touraine (France) – Description and travel
I.Title
914.4'54

Library of Congress Cataloging-in-Publication Data
Applied for.

DEDICATION

MY Dear Fellow-Traveller,—On looking back to the countless occasions
on which you have given me fruitful advice,
I begin to realise that my indebtedness to you
is fast growing beyond computation. Service
ought by rights to be repaid by service, but
I have long since abandoned all hope of ever
being able to acquit my obligations in that
way. Gratitude is now the only coin at my
disposal, so let me acknowledge my years-old
debt and the fresh increment which has been
added to it in the shape of this record of our
delightful summer in Touraine. This book
is, indeed, as much yours as mine, since it
would probably never have been written but
for your suggestion and encouragement. I
can imagine a familiar look of denegation
appearing in your brown eyes as you read
this ; but it was ever your habit to forget and

deny your good offices. Surely you recollect
a certain summer-day colloquy of ours on the
subject of the preparations necessary for such
a journey as we had undertaken, and your
remarks on the tenfold enjoyment to be got
out of travel when the mind was well-stored
with information about the places to be
visited ? " If travellers would only give as
much thought to their intellectual equipment
as to the contents of their trunks and portmanteaus," you said, amongst other things,
" they would find that these beautiful châteaux
are something more than mere conglomera-
tions of stone and mortar. Studied in connection with the times through which they
have passed, they become living entities, as
fascinating as great human personalities, and
every bit as entrancing as works of fiction."
Whilst fully agreeing with all that you said,
I ventured to point out that the ordinary
traveller was a person with limited time,
and that, whereas trunks and portmanteaus
might be got ready in a day, his intellectual
baggage could not be buckled up before the
lapse of at least five to six weeks. My own

experience in that matter had taught me a
lesson. Prior to setting out on our tour, I
had searched in vain for a book, either in
English or in French, which would give me
the facts that I thought were necessary for the
proper understanding of the châteaux of the
Loire. In the great library where I usually
browse, I found, it is true, many books on
Touraine, but, though some had excellent
points, all, to my mind, were defective.
Some were incomplete, inasmuch as many
important châteaux were not even mentioned;
others were out of date or inaccurate; and
others, again, were either too technical or
too diffuse. So I had to obtain the architectural, historical, and topographical information I needed from a multitude of
sources: unwieldy art folios, archæological
dictionaries, forgotten pamphlets, ancient
manuscripts, and the musty memoirs of
historical societies. How many travellers,
I asked, have the leisure to undertake so long
and exacting a work as this? "Few indeed,"
you replied, "though most tourists, without
an excessive amount of research, might do

a little in the way of supplementing the
meagre descriptions of their guide-books."
And then, after a pause, you added thought-
fully : "But why don't you save them the
trouble, and by writing an account of our
journey pack their 'intellectual baggage' with
all that it ought to contain?" Well, your
idea, you see, has borne fruit ; and I sincerely
trust that the manner in which it has fructified
will be at once agreeable to yourself and useful
to those who propose to follow the route
we took in the Indre-et-Loire and adjoining
departments.

On looking at the map you will observe
that our sojourn, though it was initially
intended to be a summer in Touraine,
eventually developed into a visit to several
of the ancient provinces of France. We were
out of Touraine when we started to see
the châteaux of the Loire, and at the end of
our wanderings we were again some distance
from its borders. But that must necessarily
be the case with all who set out to visit
those splendid old buildings. The name
Touraine has now become a very elastic

one, and is rarely used by the tourist in its strictly geographical sense; it is to him merely a convenient name for a certain indefinite part of central France celebrated for its historical houses and its natural beauties.

And this leads me to ask you, now that you have seen everything that the ancient province has to show, if you do not consider, with me, that it is justly celebrated? Or do you think, with Stendhal, that "la belle Touraine n'existe pas"? The author of *Le Rouge et le Noir* must have been in a particularly paradoxical mood when, recollecting the grandiose landscapes of his beloved Italy, he wrote that phrase in his amusing *Mémoires d'un Touriste*. However that may be, his words of disparagement, which we must not forget appear in one of the numerous works on which Henri Beyle's reputation is in no way based, have never done any real harm. Beautiful Touraine has continued to be every whit as popular as it was seventy to eighty years ago, at which time, according to Balzac, we English began to appreciate its qualities and descended upon it "like a cloud of grasshoppers." Moreover, as far as you and I are concerned, I think I may say that our admiration for it is not likely to abate, even though our eyes may in the future behold greater beauties. And let me add, in conclusion, that I hope the day is not far distant when you will once more be able to take to the road in company with yours affectionately,   F. L.

PARIS, *September* 1908

CONTENTS

xi

LIST OF ILLUSTRATIONS

IN COLOUR

IN MONOTONE

A SUMMER IN TOURAINE

CHAPTER I

THE FRENCH RENAISSANCE AND TWO OF ITS PALACES

I T must have been the recollection of passages in the chronicles and memoirs of certain French writers of the fifteenth and sixteenth centuries that prompted us to choose Blois as the starting-point of our wanderings on the banks of the Loire. For, as we proceeded towards our destination,— at times along roads shaded by long lines of poplars, at others alongside the river, with vineyards, golden-yellow cornfields, and stretches of waving feathery-topped asparagus ever in view,—we found ourselves travelling in company with Jean d'Auton, Jean Marot, Brantôme, and other ancient writers, and, out of fragments of their rugged yet often picturesque prose, forming an alluring picture of the days when that quiet provincial town was one of the most important centres in France.

These pleasant old writers—may you never have less agreeable fellow-travellers, or less perspicacious inspirers!—depicted Blois at the height of its fame as a royal town, with the rulers of France and a brilliant retinue in their magnificent château on the hill above the Loire. They introduced us to the daily life of the court, which was still mediæval in its taste for physical exercises,—a life largely made up of duels and wrestling-matches, jousts and tournaments, hunting and hawking excursions, and games of tennis. With companies of splendidly accoutred noblemen and archers, they took us along the roads leading to the Château of Blois to bid welcome to foreign princes and ambassadors, who, as they entered the courtyard of the palace, were received with flourishes of trumpets and clarions, and the joyous beating of tabors; and whose reception by the king and queen, surrounded by the noblest lords, ladies, and damsels of France, was the occasion for grand and imposing ceremonies. They obtained entrance for us to councils of state, and enabled us to be present at the signing of laws and treaties; and, above all, they passed before our eyes a series of portraits of men and women who exercised a preponderant influence on the manners, customs, and thought of their age.

First came Louis xii and his consort Anne of Brittany : the former a tall, thin man, sober and avaricious, but kindly in manner and endowed with a love of fine houses and beautiful tapestries ; the latter " an honourable and virtuous queen, full of wisdom, a true mother of the poor, an aid to noblemen, a protector of ladies, damsels, and girls of gentle birth, and a patron of learned men." Both, we learnt, held art and literature in honour, but Anne, unlike her utilitarian husband, loved letters for their own sake, and put him far into the shade. A gradual, broad, and subtle movement known as the Renaissance was then showing early signs of its presence in France,—that humanistic movement which Michelet well called " the discovery by man of himself and of the world,"—and her court of noble ladies and poets helped in no small measure to enlarge man's intellectual outlook and to prepare the ground for that definite loosening of his bonds which was to be the glory of the reign of Francis i. For with the cultured Francis and his gentle Queen Claude, who, to give Brantôme's own words, "was very good and very charitable, most kind to every one, and who never gave displeasure or did ill to any person either of her court or kingdom," the Renaissance came in all its brilliance. The civilisation of the Middle Ages was passing away, and giving place not only to fresh manners and customs but also to new ideals; literature, which had been despised under Louis XI and even declared to be detrimental to those following the career of arms, was regarded by soldier and civilian alike as of primary importance; and the free development of the intellect generally, as set forth in Baldassare Castiglione's *Cortegiano*, which Francis' secretary, Jacques Colin, had translated from the Italian, became the one aim of the illustrious women and prelates, nobles and wealthy commoners, literary men and artists of many nationalities, who had gathered around the king in the palace which we were rapidly approaching. And as, at last, we came within sight of that superb Château of Blois, there vividly rose before us the unforgettable figures of two of that brilliant company: the graceful poet Clément Marot and the marvellously accomplished Margaret of Angoulême, Queen of Navarre,—the two great products of the Renaissance, and the latter its very incarnation.

If on no other ground than that the Château of Blois was the scene of this epoch-making movement, you would do well, on undertaking a journey among the châteaux of the Loire, to follow our example and go there at the outset. But, apart from the fact that, on entering its courtyard, you will feel you are stepping into the atmosphere of the Renaissance, there is a special reason in your case for visiting it before any other of the châteaux of that part of France. You are bent on seeing fine buildings, and at Blois and in the surrounding country there are four of the finest to be seen anywhere,—four masterpieces of architecture, which were built (and I believe the case is unprecedented) within less than fifty years, comprising the end of the fifteenth and the beginning of the sixteenth centuries. These, naming them in the order of their construction, are : a portion of the Château of Amboise, the wing of the Château of Blois built under Louis xii, that due to Francis i and Claude of France, and the Château of Chambord. The accomplishment of so much in so short a time proves that Blois was the

centre of an important colony of architects ;
and it is there, undoubtedly, that it is most
profitable to begin to study their handiwork.

But before giving a detailed account of our
visit to Blois, let me seize the opportunity
presented by the mention of these consummate
artists of drawing attention to two points
connected with them and their work : first,
the question of their nationality, and, secondly,
that of their indebtedness to the Italian
Renaissance. The four masterpieces I have
just mentioned were for a long time attributed
to Italian architects, but the records now
make it perfectly clear that they were planned
and built by Frenchmen. Documentary
evidence apart, however, a critical comparison
between French châteaux and Italian palaces
of the Renaissance shows that they could not
be the work of men of the same nationality.
Differing in almost every particular, the
former are distinguished from the latter by
numerous architectural details of purely French
origin,—a clear indication not only that they
were not built by Italians, but also that France
owes much less to Italy than has been hitherto
claimed. Indeed, strictly speaking, it is not
quite correct to apply the word Renaissance
to the transformation which French archi-

tecture underwent in the days of Louis XII
and Francis I. For, unlike Italy, France had
by no means been in a dormant condition
since the fall of the Roman Empire. The art
of architecture, it is true, was in a state of
stagnation, owing to a too slavish respect on
the part of her architects for the threadbare
style of the Middle Ages ; but there had been
no break in that art, which only required to
be brought into touch with newer ideas to
develop and flourish anew. The Italian
campaigns of Charles VIII, Louis XII, and
Francis I supplied this much-needed inspiration, and the result was a new form of
architecture, composed of a union between
some of the traditions of the mediæval art of
France and the artistic principles underlying
the Italian Renaissance. But, though what is
known as the French Renaissance and the
Italian movement bearing the same name
sprang from a common source, it should not
be forgotten that they proceeded along
different lines, and that the fruits of the
former were so vastly dissimilar to those of
the latter, that French art as exemplified in
these royal residences of the sixteenth century
may justly be regarded as essentially national
in its character.

It is, then, the growth and final blossoming
of this art that makes the Château of Blois
so well worth a visit. Its claims upon your
interest, however, are not wholly confined, as
we soon discovered on arriving there, to the
period of the Renaissance. Almost as far
back as one can go in history, strongholds
stood on the site of the present château, and
portions of these older structures (some of
which I shall later have occasion to mention)
remain even to-day. The existing buildings
were, in all probability, preceded, first by a
Roman fortress, and then, towards the middle
of the tenth century, by a castle and residence,
built to the order of Theobald the Trickster.
During the next four centuries, various
occupants added to this feudal residence. But
they do not appear to have made it of any
great artistic worth, although Froissart,
writing about 1388, described it as "fine,
large, strong, and luxurious,—one of the most
beautiful castles in the kingdom of France."
This usually accurate and impartial chronicler
was chaplain to Guy II, Count of Blois, and
he lived in the château ; so it is not unlikely
that a desire to please his protector led him,
for once, into an exaggeration. At any rate,
we find no such high praise in Antoine

Astesan's account of a journey which he made through France some sixty years later ; for he speaks of it merely as " a château so strong and so large that it can accommodate several thousand men and horses."

Be content, therefore, to picture this earlier Château of Blois less for the sake of its plain, substantial walls than for that of the men who found protection behind them. Personally, I never think of it without summoning up at least two of those figures of the Middle Ages,—the poets Charles of Orleans and François Villon. Charles, as the successor of Louis of Orleans, Count of Blois, was its occupant from the end of the fourteenth century until 1415, the year of Agincourt, where he was taken prisoner ; and, after twenty-five years' captivity in England, he once more made it his home, to surround himself with a small court of literary noblemen and poets, to compose his polished ballads and roundelays, and to live that comfortable, lazy life which so well suited his epicurean tastes and habits. As to Villon,— Villon, the thief and assassin, yet, withal, the greatest poet and most fascinating character of his age,—the obscurity with which so many periods of his strange life are enveloped, makes it impossible to say at exactly what time and

for how long he was at Blois. But that he
really did belong to Charles' literary court,
and received from his brother poet both
payment and protection, is evident from his
poems. Was he there on December 19, 1457,
on the occasion of the birth of Charles'
daughter, Mary? And did he there and
then write the congratulatory poem *Le Dit de
la naissance Marie*, which was found carefully
preserved in a manuscript of Charles' own
works? Let me confess to a fondness for
accepting these conjectures as realities, and at
the same time to an inclination for imagining
that the relationship between the light-hearted
Charles and the bohemian " Maistre " François
was unbroken until as late as 1465. For that
was the year in which the Count of Blois died,
leaving his estates to a child of two, the future
Louis xii, who, thirty-three years later, on the
death of Charles viii, was to inaugurate a
complete transformation of the home of his
ancestors.

Louis, impelled by a deep affection for his
birthplace,—" où il avait été nourri tout son
jeune âge,"—began by building the eastern wing
of the present château, and the Chapel of Saint
Calais on the south ; Francis i and Claude of
France continued his work by adding the

northern side ; and François Mansart, in 1635,
replaced the wing erected by Louis' father on
the west by one which he built for Gaston
of Orleans. Thus, the Château de Blois of
to-day is in the form of an irregular quadrilateral. And it covers about half of the
triangular plateau, protected on all sides, which
was occupied by earlier buildings.

Seen under favourable conditions of light
(it was a perfect summer afternoon when we
visited Blois), it would be difficult to imagine
anything more delightful than the exterior
façade of the eastern wing. Facing the little
square by way of which the château is
approached,—a square which was formerly
an outer court,—it pleases for a variety of
reasons, but principally because of the exquisite harmony of its colouring, the richness
of its decoration, and the stateliness of its
lines. After the fashion of Renaissance days,
a judicious use has been made of red and black
bricks, which have the double effect of being
highly decorative and of throwing into relief
the white stone windows, the cornice, and the
balustrade. How admirably, too, the magnificent skylights, with their graceful pinnacles
and profusion of ornamentation, stand out
against the purple, high-pitched roof, which

might have been in just the slightest degree
monotonous but for the smaller wooden
skylights and the well-proportioned brick
chimneys! The groundwork of the general
decoration is composed of innumerable fleurs-
de-lis, the porcupine and festooned rope which
formed the respective devices of Louis and
Anne of Brittany, and their initials ;—the last
named being particularly noteworthy, since
such embellishments were unknown before
the end of the fifteenth century. Thus does
the eye wander from one beautiful detail to
another, until, at last, it centres in its greatest
delight : a richly ornamented niche above the
entrance, and, beneath its splendid canopy, an
equestrian statue of the King. This statue,
by the bye, is the only part of the exterior of
the eastern wing which does not date from the
sixteenth century ; it is the work of Emile
Seurre, a sculptor in whom Félix Duban, the
restorer of the château, found an exceptionally
able collaborator. Indeed, judging by an old
drawing of the statue which preceded it, and
which was destroyed at the time of the Revolution, it is even an improvement on the
original work. Considered as a whole, and
purely from the point of view of style, the
general composition of this charming façade

BLOIS: ENTRANCE TO THE CASTLE

THE CHÂTEAU OF BLOIS: EASTERN WING AND CHAPEL OF ST. CALAIS

is, of course, Gothic ; but it is Gothic architecture with the stamp of a period of transition
upon it ; a style of architecture into which
there already entered something of the feeling
of the Renaissance.

The façade facing the courtyard, which is
reached through a little door surmounted by
a porcupine, is similar in ornamentation to
the exterior front, only less luxuriant. It
possesses an arcade, with alternately round and
square pillars ; and its two extremities are
flanked by towers, containing finely ornamented staircases, which lead to the former
royal apartments. These are now used by the
town of Blois as a museum and picture-gallery.
And I may say, incidentally, that the pictures
are well worth seeing, especially the historical
portraits of the fifteenth, sixteenth, and
seventeenth centuries, including at least one
by François Clouet, who, since he was a native
of Touraine, deserves special notice. In these
rooms, too, are several highly coloured and
gilded chimney-pieces, almost wholly the
work of Duban, the originals having been so
terribly injured during the reign of Louis
XVIII that little remained as a guide to
restoration. The finest is that in the room in
which Anne of Brittany died in 1514. From

the already mentioned arcade access is gained
to the most important of the few remaining
parts of the older château,—the vast Salle des
Etats, so called because it was there that the
States-General, which had such an influence
over the destinies of France at the time of the
wars of religion, met in 1576 and 1588. It
dates from the beginning of the thirteenth
century, and is composed of two sections,
separated by a row of eight painted columns.
" A rather poor building " was Viollet-le-
Duc's description of it, and there can, indeed,
be no doubt that its present bare and altered
state gives but a faint idea of the splendour of
the original hall.

On the south side of the courtyard is a
somewhat similar arcade to that of the eastern
wing, with a smaller fifteenth century building
above it, and, adjoining, the Chapel of Saint
Calais. This chapel with elegant slate spire
is said to have been the jewel of the buildings
constructed by Louis, but its present state tells
so clear a tale of decadence that one cannot
fail to be disappointed with it. Apart from
the decay caused by time and neglect, it
suffered deliberate injury at the hands of
Gaston of Orleans, in such sort that no amount
of restoration, were it ever so conscientious or

so gorgeously carried out, could make up for
its losses.

After passing Louis' buildings in review,
two very natural questions occur to us : Who
was the architect ?   And when did he begin
his work ?   A certain Colin Byard has been
mentioned as having drawn up the plans, but,
on looking into the matter, you will find that
his claims to the honour are so slight that he
cannot seriously be regarded as their author.
Should you extend your researches to ancient
documents, the result is the same,—failure to
discover the smallest particle of conclusive
evidence in favour of any one ; so you have,
perforce, to give up the quest and confess, like
others, that the name of Louis' architect is unknown.   On the other hand, the records, incomplete though they are, reveal the names and
positions of men who saw his plans faithfully
carried out.   François de Pontbriant, the
member of a family which had long been
attached to the Dukes of Orleans, and who
had been in charge of the Château of Amboise,
was clerk of the works ; Simon Guischart was
foreman ; and Jacques Sourdeau, a native of
Loches, was master-mason.   The last-named
workman probably played a much more important rôle than appears on the surface, his

humble title of *maître-maçon*, which has not
the slightest analogy with the present significa-
tion of the word, being quite sufficient to
identify him, theoretically and practically, as
a master of the art of building. As to the
date on which he and his companions began
to execute the architect's orders, it has been
given as 1498. Here, again, however, there
is a doubt. In that year, Louis was probably
far too much occupied with his divorce from
Jeanne of France and his projected marriage
with Anne of Brittany,—not to mention
ordinary affairs of state,—to have either the
time or the inclination to think about the
building of his palace. So perhaps the following year is a more likely date for the laying
of the foundations of the eastern wing, which
was approaching completion in 1503.

The continuation of Louis' project to build
an entirely new château was due, in a great
measure, to his daughter, Claude ;—a fact
worthy of special note, since the credit for her
initiative is as richly deserved as the time it
has been withheld from her is long. Gentle
and retiring in nature as she was, she has been
overshadowed in history by her dashing
husband, whose share of glory has been quite
out of proportion to the part he took in the

construction of a building which is unrivalled in the whole of France. Both before the work was begun and whilst it was in progress, her taste and judgment undoubtedly largely came into play ; and if every one had his or her rights, it would be her name, and not that of Francis, which would be given to the northern wing of the Château of Blois.

As, on the day of our arrival, we came along the stony streets of Blois and emerged on to the Place Victor Hugo, the sight of the exterior front of this wing was our first introduction to the château. Coming upon it with fresh and eager minds, it produced a particularly vivid and lasting impression ; and we can still distinctly see it rising above the little town—with almost a personal air of majesty—from its verdure-covered base. Resplendent in the sunlight, frankly acknowledging the inspiration received from a rejuvenated Italy, and radiating the warm feeling of the unfettered art of the sixteenth century, it joyously springs aloft on portions of the old feudal castle : a masterpiece in a new style built on thirteenth century foundations, and thus a symbol, as it were, of the triumph of humanism over the dark ages preceding the Renaissance. Its dominating feature is a

2

double row of painted and gilded *loggie* extending nearly the whole of its length. Their
effect is delightful. By opening the façade
to the light and the air, they give it a certain
human touch which would have been largely,
if not wholly lacking had they been replaced
by windows. For these *loggie* were meant
for use on sunny days, especially the lower
series with their charming little balconies,
which want nothing to make them complete
save the figures of Francis, Queen Claude, and
their courtiers. Above the upper tier is a
fine row of grotesque gargoyles,—no two
alike ; and then, immediately under a broad,
low-pitched roof, partly supported by round
columns, a balcony stretching from one end
of the wing to the other, and commanding
a splendid view over the town and surrounding country. A profusion of sculptured detail,
the decoration pleases no less than the general
architecture of the façade. One device—that
found on all buildings erected by Francis—
predominates : a salamander surmounted by
a crown. Such is the exterior front of this
northern wing. Yet, after describing it, we
have a feeling that by no means everything
has been said. However minute our description may be, we have to confess that there

is something intangible about this fascinating front, some subtle spirit that emanates from things of beauty, which escapes analysis.

But, whatever might be said in praise of the beauty of this façade, how much more applicable it would be to the one on the right of the courtyard ! For the interior front, consisting of three floors, has never been surpassed, either in originality of design or in richness and ingenuity of ornamentation. Other pieces of architecture of the same period so pale in comparison that, until you have seen this example, you can form but a faint idea of what the sixteenth century was capable of producing. Where, indeed, do you find anything so perfect as its admirably proportioned windows, with their carved mullions and transoms ; its delicate stone embroidery ; its pilasters with exquisitely sculptured capitals ; its balustrade formed of the initials of Francis and Claude, interwoven with crowns, and surrounded by the festooned rope ; or its skylights adorned with the loveliest of pinnacles ? And yet, beautiful as these are individually and as a whole, they are merely the setting for a jewel of greater price. A little to the left of the middle of the façade there stands out the celebrated staircase of the Château of

Blois,—that staircase which has been well
named the final word of the art of the
Renaissance. It can best be described by
calling it a sort of cylinder placed on end
against the building,—a cylinder with inter-
stices from base to summit which leave the
winding, easily mounted steps open to the air,
—a cylinder as finely chiselled in parts as many
a precious example of the cabinet-maker's art.
The unknown sculptors whom the architect
of the northern wing engaged to carry out
this work of ornamentation—(he, too, by the
bye, is unknown,[1] though some think that
Queen Claude's choice fell upon Charles Viart,
who, in 1515, built the greater part of the
Orleans and Beaugency town-halls)—those
artists, whose handiwork has been more
durable than their names and biographies, have
covered the lower portion of the staircase with
the most varied, intricate, and beautiful designs
imaginable. The pilasters, which are decorated at their base with clear-cut medallions,
are one mass of delicate arabesques. Under
the porch and within the sunk panels beneath

---

[1] The records, however, are clear as to his collaborators.
They were the same men who worked for Louis XII—François
de Pontbriant, Simon Guischart, and Jacques Sourdeau; and
they held identically the same positions.

STAIRCASE IN THE COURTYARD AT BLOIS

the first balustrade is a similar ornamentation, and there, in addition, are more of the now familiar salamanders, and the crowned initials of the King and Queen. But the chief beauty of these pilasters resides in the adorable statues of women resting on projecting pedestals, and beneath shrine-like canopies, between the first and second balustrade, where the architect has placed them so skilfully that every attribute of their beauty is seen to advantage. These, we were told by the guide whom the municipality of Blois imposes on visitors, are by Jean Goujon. But that, of course, is an error, since the interior façade of the northern wing was built between 1515 and 1519 ; and the earliest works of the great sculptor date from much later—1540. However, though we could not sanction the attribution, we could, at any rate, accept it as a tribute to the high artistic quality of these statues, which are not unworthy even of an artist of his reputation. Above the second balustrade, beneath which, as I have already said, they stand, runs a third, with the same gentle obliquity. Both are ornamented in identically the same manner, each section between the pilasters being decorated with an F interlaced with a crown and flanked by salamanders. In this they differ

from the lower balustrade, which has balusters
of a more ordinary form, but each a piece of
delicate sculpture. Thus do bold chiselling
and minute arabesque meet the eye almost
wherever it alights ; and so I might continue
to describe them if I had any hope of doing
justice to this unique staircase. Many have
described it before me, but no one has yet
succeeded in giving an adequate idea of its
incomparable richness. As with all masterpieces, it must be seen with your own eyes if
you would fully appreciate its beauties.

Once we had ascended this staircase, but
not without lingering a little over the lacework of sculpture with which parts of its
inner walls are covered,—once we had entered
the interior of the northern wing, our vision
of a golden age of art, evoked by contemplat-
ing the fruit of one of its happiest moods,
gradually faded away. Before wholly vanish-
ing, however, it was more than once, as we
went from room to room, momentarily
quickened into fresh vividness by a few
remaining traces of Francis and Claude :
here an initialed mantelpiece, gorgeous with
blue and gold ; there a doorway embellished
with characteristic sixteenth century cupids,
birds, and flowers in low-relief ; and here,

again, a room panelled with exquisitely carved
wood. Of the ancient splendours of those
former royal apartments, these are all that are
left, and, alas! they were insufficient to keep
the times of the man and woman who inspired
them before our mental eye. Moreover, little
indeed as those rooms lend themselves to
musing, so chilling to the imagination is their
bare unfurnished state, so much at variance
with one's æsthetic sense is the crude brilliancy
with which a too conscientious restorer has
coloured their walls, we found them too
crowded with memories of Francis' successors
to permit us to form an effective picture of
the heyday of humanism. They recalled
the brief reign of Henry II when the strife
between Catholic and Huguenot was making
its first appearance; they recalled the Regency
of Catherine de' Medici, darkened by the
wars of religion and St. Bartholomew's day;
and, above all, they recalled the sinister days
of the weak and treacherous Henry III, whose
dramatic conflict with the Duke of Guise
over the question of a successor to the throne
ended in assassination. Their very nomen-
clature is proof of how imperatively they
recall these three rulers. The rooms on
the second storey, consisting of a *salle des fêtes*

and a guardroom, which occupy the portion
of the wing facing the courtyard, are named
the apartments of Henry II.   On the side overlooking the Place Victor Hugo are Catherine
de' Medici's drawing-room, the bedroom in
which she died early in 1589, an oratory, a
study, and two other smaller rooms.   This
study is the one whose wood panelling dates
from the reign of Francis; it contains no
fewer than two hundred and thirty-seven
panels, all differently carved; and behind
some of them are skilfully concealed hiding-
places.   The ceiling and mantelpiece are the
work of Duban, who, instead of executing
them in keeping with the pure Renaissance
style of the rest of the room, was inspired
by woodwork at the Château of Beauregard,
dating from the period of Henry III.   After
each of these works of art had been pointed
out, the guide invited us to look from the
windows on to the square, and told her oft-
repeated tale of the escape, in 1619, of Marie
de' Medici, who was exiled to Blois by her
son at the instigation of the Duke of Luynes.
Our fellow-visitors, gazing into the depths
below, received the narration of this remarkable example of feminine intrepidity with
many exclamations of surprise, which would

have been fully justified if only the story had been correct. But, as a fact, Mary and her rope-ladder never dangled from those northern windows. She effected her escape by means of ladders on the southern side, and did it with comparative ease, since in her day there existed no such high parapets as those which now surround the château on three of its sides. Our cicerone's error was, however, excusable on the score of this minor detail of history having been inaccurately recorded even by serious historians, and to do her justice it must be said that her account of the dramatic incidents which occurred in the rooms on the third storey was, on the whole, more in accordance with historical truth. These rooms are called the apartments of Henry III, and their distribution is almost identical with that of the lower floor ; two guardrooms look on to the courtyard, and on the opposite side of the building are the King's drawing-room, his bedroom, and a dressing-room. Our interest, naturally, was centred almost entirely on the bedroom, for it was there that the final scene in the murder of the Duke of Guise was enacted at the close of the year 1588. For some time before the crime was committed Henry had decided

to kill the Duke, whose existence as leader
of the Catholic party which was trying to
force the King to choose another successor
to the throne than the rightful one—Henry of
Bourbon, King of Navarre, the head of the
Huguenots—was a constant menace to his
crown and his own life. The day fixed
for the murder was December 23. At four
o'clock in the morning the King had forty-
five of his most faithful courtiers stationed in
a private staircase to lie in wait for the victim.
On arriving at the council meeting, which
Guise attended every morning at eight
o'clock, the King's secretary informed the
Duke that his master wished to speak to
him in his room ; and it was whilst on his
way there by a necessarily circuitous route—
Henry having had a doorway walled up—that
he was attacked and, after a terrible struggle,
stabbed to death. Assisted by a recollection of the narratives of Miron and other
chroniclers, we pictured the scene—the
Duke's suspicion, on hearing footsteps behind
him, that he had been led into a trap, his cry
of " Mercy on me ! " as he received the first
dagger-thrust, his bare-handed fight against
the forty-five armed men, his slowly declining
resistance as he lost blood from his wounds,

his death at the very foot of the King's
bedstead, and the figure of Henry with his
ear against the door anxiously listening to
the sounds of the struggle.   How grimly
tragic is that last incident !—verily as tragic
as the picture which Walter Savage Landor
draws for us in his imaginary conversation
between the Empress Catherine and Princess
Dashkof, who listened to the murder of the
Emperor of Russia from an adjoining room.
When the heavy thud of the Duke's body
came to the King's ears he slowly opened
the door, and, thrusting his pale face into the
room, took in at a glance the scene of the
murder.   The body of the Duke of Guise
was stretched without movement at the foot
of the bed.   " Do you think that he is dead ? "
asked Henry.   " I think so, Sire," replied
the chief of the murderers, raising the victim's
head ; "for he has the colour of death."
Then only did Henry dare to approach and
look on the face of his dead enemy.   " Mon
Dieu ! " he exclaimed ; " what a size he is !
He looks even bigger dead than living ! "
Then he pushed the body with his foot.
Estoile states that he even kicked the dead
man's face, an insult which Guise is said to
have inflicted upon the body of the Admiral

de Coligny sixteen years before. But though
Guise was dead, Henry's fears for his personal
safety were by no means allayed. On the
following day he had the Duke's brother,
the Cardinal of Lorraine, murdered in the
tower which terminates the wing of Francis I
on the west. Not many days after these two
murders, a third death, but a natural one this
time, took place in the château—the death of
Catherine de' Medici. Brantôme, who wrote
a eulogy of that great yet unscrupulous
woman, says that she died from sorrow at
the thought of having contributed to the crimes
by " heedlessly bringing the princes to the
palace." " ' Alas ! Madame,' replied the
Cardinal of Bourbon, ' you have heedlessly
led us all to the slaughter ! ' And that
remark, coupled with the death of those
poor men, so touched her heart that she
took to her bed, having previously been
ill, and never rose from it again."

In the eyes of the Kings of France, these
two murders would appear to have cast an
indelible blot on the fair name of the Château
of Blois, for henceforth not a single one cared
to inhabit it. Moreover, after the death of
Henry III in 1589—a victim in his turn of
the assassin's knife—only one more Duke

THE CHÂTEAU OF BLOIS

of Orleans chose it as a home, and that was the brother of Louis XIII, Gaston by name, who, in addition to being singularly insensible to beauty, was too obtuse to be affected by sanguinary memories. He it was who employed François Mansart to build the western wing, that cold, but stately building which faces you on entering the courtyard. Though a fine example of that architect's work, it left no other impression on our minds save a feeling of thankfulness that Gaston of Orleans did not pull down the other wings of the château and rebuild them in the formal style of his own day. That such was actually his intention is plain from the plans and sections published by Blondel.

After Gaston's death in 1660, when the château became the property of Louis XIV, its history as a royal residence rapidly drew to a close, only two members of royalty ever again occupying it,—namely, Mary Casimir, widow of John Sobieski, King of Poland, and the mother of King Stanislaus, who died there in 1722. Then came a period of decadence. It was offered for sale in 1774 and 1778, but without finding a purchaser, so the King in 1788 ordered its destruction! Fortunately the Revolution saved it from such an igno-

minious end, though the men of 1789 can by no
means be exonerated from the blame of having
committed many acts of vandalism both inside
and outside the palace. Used as a barracks
until 1842, the château—like the Palace of
the Popes at Avignon, the Château of Nantes,
and other fine old French buildings—suffered
further injury from military hands. At last,
lovers of architecture saw the necessity first
of preservation and secondly of restoration ;
and the latter task — a most difficult and
delicate one in the then existing state of
the building—was begun in 1845, under the
direction of Félix Duban, and continued until
1870, the year in which this zealous architect
completed his last work, the decoration of the
Chapel of Saint Calais.

Of the four masterpieces which I have
already said are to be seen at Blois and in the
surrounding country two had now revealed
their beauties to us. Knowing that a close
connection existed between one of them, the
northern wing of the Château of Blois, and
one of the others yet to be visited, the Château
of Chambord, we decided to make this third
example of Renaissance architecture the object of our next excursion, and to leave the
fourth, the Château of Amboise, for a later

occasion during our sojourn on the banks of the Loire.

Blois and Chambord are associated, of course, through Francis, who, not satisfied with continuing his predecessor's work, felt a desire to build a palace which he could call entirely his own. His choice of a site was from some points of view unfortunate ; for he selected a marshy valley, watered by the little river Cosson, in the arid district known as the Sologne, some eleven miles from Blois. As so many other more suitable places for a royal house might have been found, it has been conjectured that this preference for one of the dreariest districts in France was dictated by the fact that a lady whom he had loved in his youth had a manor in the same neighbourhood. But that is a rather far-fetched suggestion, and it seems much more likely that he chose the site because it was on the outskirts of the forest of Boulogne, and in consequence eminently suited for indulging his well-known love of the chase.

One morning in mid July, before the sun had had time to make travelling irksome, we set out thither. Our road lay alongside the Loire, then but a puny stream placidly flowing in a broad uneven bed of yellow sand, dotted

in parts with shallow pools, or bordered with
rivulets which meandered here and there to
join, at times, the narrow central channel.
Whatever it might be farther down towards
the sea, it was far from being at this part of
its course the river "large comme un lac" of
which Balzac writes in one of his short
stories; and no one, unless he had an inkling
as to its character for capriciousness, would
ever have thought that so peaceful a looking
stream had inspired terror in the hearts of
generations of farmers.   But the very highway
whence a fine prospect of its course is obtained
clearly indicates its redoubtable nature.   This
road winds along the top of a high, broad embankment, originally constructed under Louis
the Debonair, though not completed in its
present state until the days of Philip the Fair,
—an embankment whose purpose is manifest.
Should you chance to be in Touraine at a
particularly wet season, you will have an
ocular demonstration of the invaluable services
it can render.   After a few hours' heavy rain
the sandy bed of the Loire is no longer visible;
a week's steady downpour will see the yellow
waters, now racing along with the swiftness of
a mill stream, half-way up that twenty-foot
buttress; and in a month to six weeks they

will be level with the top, if they have
not actually broken it down and flooded the
valley for miles around.   That has frequently
happened, and tens of thousands of pounds'
damage has resulted, hence the reputation of
the Loire for being one of the most erratic
and troublesome rivers in France.   We
followed it for nearly seven miles, passing
the eighteenth century Château of Ménars,
whose terraced gardens pleasantly descend the
opposite bank.   Then we branched off from
the river to the right, passed through the
hamlets of Montlivault and Maslives, traversed
cornfields and vineyards, and at length reached
one of the entrances to the domain of
Chambord.

A long straight woodland avenue leads
direct to the château, glimpses of which were
obtained through the trees as we approached.
Finally the entire huge construction came into
view and positively seemed to crush us with
its immensity.   At the first glance, I thought
of Viollet-le-Duc's description of it and felt
how true it was.   Chambord is, indeed, a
" colossal caprice."   At the same time, it was
impossible not to admire the magnificent scale
on which it is built and the beauty of its
aerial forest of towers, domes, campaniles,

3

dormer-windows, and chimneys, with their wealth of ornamentation. A "colossal caprice" if you will, but one with the unmistakable stamp of genius upon it.

On attentively looking at this extraordinary building, it will be seen that it is composed of two structures, one above the other. The first consists of its outer walls with their large round towers, the feudal dwelling behind them, and the lordly manor ; the second is the building above the terraces. To use the words of the great architect whom I have just quoted, it was an attempt on the part of the man who built it " to unite two programmes originating in two opposed principles, —an attempt to combine in a single edifice a fortified castle of the Middle Ages and a pleasure palace. We admit that the experiment was absurd. But the French Renaissance, in literature, science, and art, was full of such hesitations at its outset ; it did not advance without sometimes casting a look of regret behind it ; it wished to free itself from the past and yet feared to break away from tradition." Bearing the impress of its age, it is likewise stamped with the image of the king who inspired it. Francis was, in truth, a strange mixture of the barbarian and the man

THE CHÂTEAU OF CHAMBORD

CHAMBORD: A PORTION OF THE DOUBLE STAIRCASE

of culture, and a good deal of his character can be read in the architecture of Chambord. Having once settled on the plan for the palace, he set to work with extraordinary energy, in 1519, to execute it, and it is recorded that for about twelve years eighteen hundred workmen were busily engaged carrying out his wishes. His architects are supposed to have been Pierre Nepveu, also known by the name of Trinqueau, and Denis Sourdeau, the son of Jacques Sourdeau, who himself has received credit for a share in the work. But it is quite possible that others whose names have not been transmitted to posterity may have had as equal a right to fame as these. Perhaps, as M. Joseph de Croÿ suggests in his volume of documents relating to the royal residences of the Loire, the rôle of architect was filled " not by a single person but by a sort of collaboration, resulting from the royal incentive, the inspiration of artists who have remained anonymous, and the practical science of incomparable workmen." Many of the records which would have thrown light on this question having been made into cartridge cases in the Year V and blown to pieces on battlefields, it will probably remain a debatable one. Francis' original intention was to con-

struct only the group of buildings called the
Donjon, but his ideas grew as the building
progressed, and first one, then another part
was added. The wings which prolong
and surround the central block came first, and
shortly after the galleries, the huge Lantern, and
the terraces. It was a gigantic and complicated
enterprise, and one whose practical difficulties
would have been a stumbling-block to the
keenest intelligence.

Our inspection of the interior of the château
began by a visit to the guardroom, which is
in the form of a Greek cross and occupies
the entire ground-floor. Each of its arms is
fifty feet long and more than thirty feet broad.
At the point where they meet, the well-known
double staircase—a constant source of wonder
and amusement to visitors—rises through the
centre of the building. It has two flights of
steps, so that people can ascend and descend
without meeting, though they are not prevented from catching a glimpse of each other
through windows in the hollow newel ;—a
most convenient arrangement, we agreed, in the
case of disunited lovers, and one which must
have many times been taken advantage of by
lords and ladies since the days of Francis.
The merit of this curious invention cannot,

by the bye, be attributed to the builders of
Chambord, for two similar staircases, dating
from the fifteenth century, existed, and I
believe still exist in Paris. Ascending one of
the spirals, we reached, on the first storey, a
second guardroom, which originally formed
part of that on the ground-floor, and, a floor
higher, the terraces. This, however, did not
mark the end of our ascent. The staircase is
surmounted by an immense structure, called
the Lantern (a copy of the ancient one),
which, in addition to being over thirty yards
high, is tipped with a colossal fleur-de-lis. A
narrow staircase leads almost to the summit,
whence a view of the surrounding country,
even as far as Blois, can be obtained on a
clear day. After each locality had in turn
been identified, we descended to the roof and
walked about in its complication of terraces and
balconies, amidst its multitudinous chimneys
and gables, ornamented with all the exuberance of the sculptural art of the Renaissance.
Whilst thus occupied the figure of Francis
naturally loomed large in our imagination,
for we could not forget that these terraces,
with their shady nooks and corners, had been
his favourite promenade, and the place where
he loved to sit on summer evenings and admire

his aerial palace. Somewhere there, in all
probability, he sat in March 1545, when,
prematurely aged, his doctors ordered him
rest, little suspecting as he mused that that
was to be his last visit to Chambord. He
left in the following May and died less than
two years later. On our return to the interior
of the château we were still thinking of his
picturesque personality, and especially when
in a little room, which was either his bedroom
or study, near the eastern tower. Its arched
ceiling is composed of sunk panels containing
F's, salamanders, fleurs-de-lis, and cupids; at
each end, in semicircular panels, are bas-
reliefs representing cupids supporting the
escutcheon of France surrounded by the
Badge of Saint Michel; and its admirably
preserved door is likewise ornamented with
the King's familiar initial and emblem. It
was on the left hand side of this room, near
the window, according to Brantôme, that the
amorous Francis, in a moment of pique at
the fickleness of some fair lady, wrote the
concise judgment :

"Toute femme varie,"

a quotation, probably, from a song of the day.
The way in which certain highly imaginative

CHAMBORD : THE TERRACES

historians of Chambord have distorted this simple story is remarkable. One has changed the King's sentence into the couplet :

> "Souvent femme varie,
> Mal habil' qui s'y fie,"

and says it was written with a diamond on a window-pane ; whilst others, who give the variant :

> "Souvent femme varie,
> Bien fol est qui s'y fie,"

have declared that the window upon which it was scratched was removed by Louis XIV in order that it might not hurt the feelings of Mlle. de la Vallière ! What a deal of trouble some writers do take over unnecessary embellishment ! In our opinion, at any rate, that charming little study required nothing more than its visible signs of Francis' former presence and the recollection of Brantôme's historiette, which he heard from the lips of one of the King's old valets, to make it thoroughly interesting. As to the other rooms of the château, I wish I could say that the attractions of the five or six (out of a total of three hundred and sixty-five) which are shown to visitors are equally satisfying. We were shown a dining-room containing a model

park of artillery,—one of the playthings of
the infant Duke of Bordeaux, who, when
Count of Chambord, had a chance of becoming the King of France,—and a collection
of portraits, principally of royal personages ; a
drawing-room filled with other uninteresting
Bourbon portraits ; a bedroom ornamented
with eighteenth century woodwork and hung
with more canvases, including a portrait of
Marie Leszcynyski, attributed to Van Loo ;
a modern bedroom containing a bed specially
made for the Count of Chambord when he
should ascend the French throne as Henry v,
but in which he never slept ; and a council
chamber hung with most unartistic tapestries
worked by enthusiastic royalist ladies and
containing a throne, made at Blois, on which
the uncrowned King was never to sit. In the
light of history, how full of irony some of
these dead things do appear,—as truly ironical
as the four gala carriages prepared for the
coronation of Henry v, and still preserved at
Chambord, but which you are permitted to
see only by special authorisation !

After the death of Francis, the building of
Chambord was continued by Henry ii, as his
initial and emblem on certain parts of the
château show ; but neither he nor his im-

mediate successors completed it. Charles IX
contributed his share. So did Catherine de'
Medici, but only as regards restoration, being,
presumably, too deeply engrossed in the study
of astrology—she nightly consulted the stars
from the Lantern during her frequent visits
to the palace—to undertake more important
work. But Henry III and Henry IV accomplished even less, the latter preferring to
reside in Paris, or at Saint Germain, or at
Fontainebleau. During the greater part of
the reign of Louis XIII and until 1660, the
château belonged to Gaston of Orleans, who,
when holding his little court there, divided
his time between hunting and playing hide-
and-seek with his daughter in the double
staircase. Then came a period — brilliant
enough in its way—when Chambord underwent changes. Louis XIV employed Mansart
to build additional wings, such as the façade
which so unfortunately masks the southern
front; but the plans, happily, were never
wholly carried out. A scheme of interior
restoration was more satisfactorily executed,
and transformed the rooms into a fitting
setting for the brilliant gatherings which the
King held there during his reign. Among
these fêtes was a very noteworthy event in

the history of dramatic art ; in September
1669, and October 1670, in the presence of
the King, the first performances were given
by Molière and his company of actors of
Monsieur de Pourceaugnac and *Le Bourgeois
Gentilhomme.* For this purpose one of the
arms of the guardroom, that on the northern
side of the first-floor, was converted into a
theatre.　In the eighteenth century Chambord
was the residence of Stanislaus Leszcynyski,
the exiled King of Poland, and of Marshal
de Saxe.　The Revolution then swept down
upon it, declared it national property, and
sought to find a purchaser for it, but without
success,—a result which was not at all surprising, considering that almost everything of
value in its multitudinous rooms had been
scattered to the winds.　In 1809, Napoleon,
who preserved it from falling into ruins,
presented it to Berthier, Prince of Wagram,
together with an annuity of £20,000, which
was to be used in maintaining it in a good
state of repair.　Louis xviii having suppressed
this annuity, Berthier's widow asked for per-
mission to sell a property which she was
quite unable to keep up.　Consequently, on
March 5, 1821, it was sold for £61,680 to
the trustees of a national subscription, which

had been started by Count Adrien de Calonne
for the purpose of presenting it to the Duke
of Bordeaux, the prospective King of France,
then a child only a little over a year old.
For more than half a century Chambord
belonged to the Duke, who changed his title
in recognition of the gift. But he did not
visit it more than twice, and he was too poor
to carry out its much-needed restoration. On
his death, in 1883, it was found that he had
bequeathed the domain to his nephews, the
Duke of Parma and the late Count of Bardi.
The contents of his will caused some dissatisfac-
tion in France, where the almost general feeling
was that the Count had "forgotten" to return
to France a typically French château. Within
the past twenty years, Chambord, which
yields a revenue of close upon £6000, has
undergone extensive restoration ; about £8000
a year is spent upon it, and up to the present
a total of nearly £80,000 has been expended.
As to whether such lavish expenditure is
justifiable may, perhaps, be open to doubt,
though, so long as preservation against the
effects of time is the only object in view, no
one, I think, will have much ground for
criticism. But it would be otherwise if an
attempt were made to make this Brobding-

nagian palace habitable for future generations of Bourbon princes, for one cannot conceive how its cheerless interiors and its draughty galleries, not to mention its by no means perfect situation, could ever be brought into line with modern ideas of comfort. As a permanent place of residence, in fact, its day is over ; it will never be more than a convenient *pied-à-terre* during the shooting season.

With many kindred reflections on the past and present of the Château of Chambord did we once more set out on our travels. As we went through the forest towards Bracieux, we took a last look at the confused mass of its grey towers and chimneys, silhouetted against a clear blue sky, and unanimously agreed that, though not so interesting either architecturally or historically as the Château of Blois, it was, nevertheless, a marvellous product of a marvellous age, and at the same time a touching monument of the ancient régime.

CHAPTER II

IN THE SAD SOLOGNE: AT CHEVERNY AND LASSAY

PLEASANTER surroundings than those amidst which we passed when travelling through the forest of Boulogne we had not up to then experienced. There was something to gratify nearly all the senses that warm summer afternoon. The air was redolent of pines; the roadside was purple with heather; and gentle woodland sounds fell soothingly upon the ear—the flutter of wings in the boughs, the call of a startled bird, the rustling of hidden things in the undergrowth, or the distant stroke of a woodman's axe. For close upon five miles did the straight shady road take us through the forest, and for nearly half an hour was our mood attuned to that of the Spirit of the Woods. Then both scene and mood changed. Receding farther and farther as we were from the Loire, we knew, however, that that was inevitable,

and that once the forest was left behind we
should meet with landscape which would
be as mournful as our sylvan highway was
exhilarating. Full of regret we emerged from
the avenue,—full of regret, but with our
spirits fortified, as against a necessary evil,
and, descending into the valley of the river
Beuvron, reached the little village of Bracieux
and the sad Sologne.

We had heard and read much about the
Sologne, but until we actually met it face to
face we did not fully realise what a cheerless
district it is. Its wind-swept plains, in many
parts covered with innumerable marshy lakes
and ponds, cannot exactly be described as

> "Wastes too bleak to rear
> The common growth of earth, the foodful ear,"

considering how much has been done since
the middle of the last century, by drainage
and the planting of hundreds of thousands
of pine trees, to render them susceptible of
cultivation. But at one time Wordsworth's
lines would have been perfect in their applica-
tion to the Sologne,—if they cannot, even
now, be appropriately used in speaking of
certain portions of it which are either still
unreclaimed or rebellious to the arts of man.

This refractory character of its soil makes it
a most striking contrast to fertile Touraine,
every scrap of which is so carefully cultivated
as often to give it the appearance of a huge
market-garden ; and it is a question whether,
with its clayey substratum, which imprisons
the rain-water near the surface and forms
fever-breeding pools, it will ever be otherwise.
Yet it is a curious fact that its area of three
thousand square miles was at one time, far
back in history, both better adapted for agri-
culture and healthier than it is to-day. It
was then covered with extensive forests, which
sucked up a considerable quantity of the
water of the marshes, and thus did man
a double service,—which he was incapable,
as it happened, of appreciating. For he set
to work to cut down the trees in time
of peace, and to burn them in time of
war, and in this way gradually converted a
district which Nature had made fairly decent
into the arid, fever-stricken spot it was so
comparatively recently—a district noted for its
high death-rate and its weak and stunted population. Fortunately the last fifty to sixty
years have seen a great improvement in
the Sologne, largely owing to the growing of
health-giving pine forests. Nevertheless, it

still remains a desolate land, a most unin-
viting one for travellers unless, as was our
own case, they have compensatory objects
in view.

We had, in fact, made up our minds to see
two other châteaux before returning to Blois
and descending the Loire : the Château of
Cheverny and the Château du Moulin, near
Lassay, whose attractions we had heard
mentioned more than once. " It is worth
travelling through many Solognes," some one
had said, " to see two such charming old
houses." So we had resolutely faced these
dreary plains of Central France. As will be
seen we were amply rewarded. After covering
some six miles of uninteresting country, we
reached the end of the first part of our journey,
Cour-Cheverny and Cheverny, twin villages in
a wooded valley, a veritable oasis in the desert.
Well advanced though the afternoon was,
there was yet time to visit the château, whose
park gates we found were opposite the church,
which itself is worthy of note both on account
of its picturesque old wooden porch and the
memorial tablets to members of the family
to whom we owe that delightful manor-
house.

The Château of Cheverny, which is built

in the style that reached its height under Louis xiv, but certain of whose details date from the close of the Renaissance, faces a long, broad avenue and a park planted with centennial trees. Within the shadow of its light and elegant façade, ornamented with marble and stone busts, standing in niches, are wide, green lawns and banks of flowers, the whole forming an ideal setting for a mansion which, unlike Chambord, has been put to its proper use since the day it was constructed.

But if its exterior and its grounds are attractive, how much more so did we find its homely interior ! With perfect courtesy we were shown, on the ground-floor, a corridor and dining-room decorated with painted panels representing scenes in the life of Don Quixote, the work of one of the numerous famous artists who have been natives of the valley of the Loire. Their author, Jean Mosnier, was born at Blois in 1600, and came of a family which had already shown a pronounced taste for art, both his father and grandfather being painters on glass. The former gave him his early lessons in painting ; but his more serious training, extending over eight years, was received in Italy, where he became a friend

4

of Poussin, and was due to the generosity
of Marie de' Medici, who, when exiled in
the château of his native town, was so struck
with a copy of Andrea Solario's " Vierge au
coussin vert," which the young painter had
made for her, that she defrayed the cost of
his education. On returning to France he
would appear to have had no reason to
complain of lack of commissions. For he
did a number of decorative paintings for
the Luxembourg Palace ; an important series
for the Bishop of Chartres' chapel and apartments ; and numerous other works (in addition to those at Cheverny and at the Château
of Valençay) for houses at Chinon, Nogent-le-
Rotrou, Saumur, and Tours. The Cheverny
decorations—and I am now referring not
merely to his Don Quixote series but to the
whole of the numerous paintings which he did
for the château—were executed when he was
at the height of his powers, and they give, to
quote the words of Philippe de Chennevières,
the author of a book on the provincial
painters of France, " a true and splendid idea
of the decorative magnificence of some of the
French châteaux of the seventeenth century."
In a beautiful state of preservation, they have
undergone little restoration, as can easily be

THE CHÂTEAU DE CHEVERNY

A ROOM AT THE CHÂTEAU DE CHEVERNY

seen on close examination. There is a marked
difference between the ancient and the modern
work; the old paint presents a rougher
surface and is richer in colour, whereas the
new has not much more in its favour than
the technical skill with which it has been
applied. Largely, however, as Mosnier's
paintings contribute to the rich colouring
of the dining-room and other rooms on the
ground-floor, other works of art play an
important part in the general scheme of
decoration, and these must be mentioned
before describing the apartments on the first-
floor. In the dining-room, whose walls are
covered with beautiful Cordova leather, stamped
with a pattern in red and gold, and whose chairs
are upholstered in the same material, is a fine
Henry IV mantelpiece with a bust of Le
Grand Monarque; the drawing-room contains
a mantelpiece ornamented with bas-reliefs of
nymphs holding wreaths above their heads,
in some respects identical with one by
Germain Pilon in the Louvre; and in other
smaller rooms is a choice collection of portraits
of the Hurault family by Clouet, Porbus,
Mignard, and Largillière.

A staircase of white embroidered stone, as
pure and as clear-cut as when it received the

finishing touches of its unknown sculptor, a
certain F. L. whose initials, with the date
1634, are to be seen on a cartouche amidst the
ornamentation, leads to the first storey.   Here
is an apartment, consisting of a guardroom,
bedroom, and other smaller rooms, and known
as the King's Apartment, which contains the
château's most finely decorated rooms.   In
the guardroom the doors, wainscoting, panels
of the shutters and ceiling form one mass of
harmonious decoration,—a mass of figures,
arabesques,   flowers,   and   Latin   mottoes.
Mosnier strove to make every stroke of his
brush symbolic, and how well and charmingly
he succeeded you will see if you take the
trouble to read his lines and discover the
meaning of his floral designs.   On one of
the panels of the wainscot we noticed a tulip
with   the   accompanying   words :   NIL   NISI
FLORE PLACET.   That was perfectly straight-
forward, for everybody knows that this flower
is only agreeable to look upon.   But we were
not so quick in finding a solution to the
painter's choice of the tulip, rather than any
other flower whose odour is also not agreeable ;
it took us a minute or two to remember that
he decorated this room at a time when tulip-
growing, introduced by the Dutch, was the

fashion in France. The symbolism of a daffodil, and the motto MEI ME PERDIDIT ARBOR was again quite clear,—or we had forgotten the story of the son of Cephisus and his metamorphosis into a narcissus. A sunflower and the words ARMA GERO COMITIS— " I bear the arms of a count "—was a fairly transparent allusion to the arms of the Counts of Cheverny. The painting which gave us most trouble was one of a trumpet-creeper, with the inscription : ADVENA CHARVS HOSPITI —" A foreigner, dear to its host "; and we should never, perhaps, have solved the problem had not a botanical friend informed us that this plant was imported into France from America in Mosnier's day, and that evidently he foresaw it would become a favourite with French horticulturists. When the novelty of unravelling these floral conundrums had somewhat worn off we turned our attention to other things, and found much to interest us, notably a fine painting of " Venus and Adonis," by Mosnier, over a mantelpiece ornamented with caryatides and statues in gilded wood, and a Flemish tapestry representing the " Abduction of Helen." Then we passed into the adjoining Chambre du Roi, which I have no hesitation in saying is the most

interesting room in the château. With the
exception of a single painting, it has lost
nothing of its original decoration, and both
Mosnier's works and the magnificent Beauvais
tapestries, representing the "Adventures of
Ulysses," look as fresh as though they had
been painted and made but yesterday. The
paintings on the ceiling and above the richly
carved mantelpiece and door depict scenes in
the story of Perseus, whilst those on the panels,
numbering no fewer than thirty, are devoted
to the love story of Theagenës and Charicleia.
Mosnier evidently had a great fondness for
Heliodorus' erotic romance, for he twice took
his inspiration from it, once at Cheverny
and once when working for the Bishop of
Chartres. This royal bed-chamber also contains an ancient bedstead and a curious old
chest which is said to have been the *coffre de
voyage* of Henry IV.

Such are the chief characteristics of the
Château of Cheverny. There now remains
but little more to be said except a few words
about the family which built it and about
certain other owners who must not be
overlooked, since they helped in no small
measure to preserve its beauties intact. The
exact date at which its founders, a Breton

family of the name of Hurault, settled in the district of Blois, is unknown, but it was some time about the end of the fourteenth century. It is known for certain, however, that at the beginning of the sixteenth century General Raoult Hurault built a house at Cheverny on the site now occupied by the outbuildings of the present château ; that it was in this house, in 1528, that the famous chancellor, Philippe Hurault, who considerably enlarged the estate, was born ; and that his eldest son, the second Count of Cheverny, pulled down part of the buildings erected by his ancestors and built the existing mansion. The exact date of its construction was 1634, and its plans were drawn up by Boyer, an architect of Blois, who in all probability was assisted in his work by many well-known sculptors of the period. After the death of the Count, who had no male issue, the house and lands surrounding it became the property of his younger daughter, Elizabeth, the wife of the Marquis de Montglas. At the beginning of the eighteenth century their descendants sold it to a lady named d'Harcourt, who in turn disposed of it to Count Dufort de Saint Leu, Lieutenant-General to the King, who made him Count of Cheverny. But the magnificent

hospitality with which the new owner entertained at the château so diminished his
fortune that at his death his son and heir was
obliged to sell the property. It was bought
by Count Jean Pierre Germain, a wealthy
banker, but again sold, this time to a M.
Guillot and his son. Two years afterwards
M. Guillot *père* died. His son married, but,
having no children to whom to leave the
château, he and his wife were struck with
the generous idea of offering it to the descendants of the family which had built it, in
order to preserve it from falling into unworthy
hands. Accordingly, in 1825, it was purchased by the Marquise de Hurault de Vibraye
for her son, the Marquis Paul de Vibraye,
who showed himself eminently worthy of
possessing so splendid a house. He it was,
in fact, who undertook its restoration,—and
intelligent restoration, too, for he was both an
archæologist and an artist. Indeed, this repre-
sentative of a great family was in knowledge
and accomplishments far above the average of
country gentlemen. In addition to restoring
his residence to its original condition, and to
transforming large tracts of waste ground
on his estate into fruitful agricultural and
forest land, he was busily occupied for more

than forty years in forming valuable miner-
alogical, geological, and other collections,
including a number of objects relating to
the study of primitive man. He died in
1878, leaving the château to his eldest son,
the Marquis Henri Hurault de Vibraye, its
present owner.

From Cheverny to Lassay, which lies a
little way off the main road from Blois to
Romorantin amidst characteristic Sologne
scenery, is a distance of about twelve miles.
When we had already covered ten of them we
reached the village of Mur, a more important
place than the neighbouring hamlet of Lassay,
and, consequently, better able to provide
accommodation for travellers. Night had
fallen. Manifestly it was then too late to
make use of our letter of introduction to the
owner of the Château du Moulin, even if
dinner at an inviting inn had not imperatively
summoned us to table. So we prepared to do
justice to what the landlord assured us was
the best that Mur could offer, and gladly fell
in with his numerous suggestions to make us
comfortable for the night. But at the close
of that simple yet admirably cooked meal, all
desire for repose, as far as I was concerned,
had vanished ; on the contrary, an irresistible

longing to be out under the stars in the then
pleasantly cool summer air, and to stretch my
legs along country roads, came upon me.
Therefore, whilst my friend retired to rest,
I sauntered forth. The village was almost
asleep. Only a few lights twinkled here and
there from cottage windows, or streamed in
a flood through the open door of a *cabaret*.
Soon I came to the last of the houses and
entered the open country. After walking for
not far short of an hour, ruminating on what
we had seen during the day, I suddenly caught
sight, between some trees and in the light of
the moon, of a glint of water and the dim
outline of a building. A dozen yards farther
brought it into fuller view, and at the same
time I recognised that the Château du
Moulin, surrounded by its moat, was before
me.

In the case of every ancient building there
is one particular hour of the day when it
looks better than at any other. One will
impress you most when seen in full sunlight ;
another should be viewed in the gray of
evening ; and a third will be in greatest
accord with its dominant characteristic in the
subdued light of a melancholy autumn day.
It is no man's good fortune, alas ! to see every

THE CHÂTEAU DU MOULIN

one exactly under its right aspect; he must leave this question of time to be decided by Fate, and consider himself lucky if, now and then, his visit coincides with the happy hour. Thus had my impromptu nocturnal excursion led me to hit on the ideal moment for seeing the Château du Moulin. Darkly reflected in the placid moonlit water of the moat, its character as a perfect type of the feudal manor-house could not have been more strikingly emphasised. Its graceful towers and pinnacles rising into a luminous sky sown with stars, a dark background of trees, the moon overhead, and their counterpart in the mysterious water, formed so romantic a picture that I should have been tempted to have compared it to a scene on the stage had I not recognised that the most skilful theatrical *mise-en-scène* could never attain such a degree of poetry or such exquisite chiaroscuro.

As I continued to gaze on this beautiful sight, memories of the builder of the château and of olden times sprang up one by one. Philippe du Moulin, a simple but wealthy squire, the descendant of a certain Jehan du Molin, had decided to build a house suitable to his station, and had chosen Jacques de

Persigny as his architect. It was the year 1480. Ten years later he had been granted a charter by Charles, Count of Angoulême and Lord of Romorantin, authorising him to fortify his manor - house with " towers, barbicans, loop-holes for cannon, for crossbow-men, and for archers, drawbridge, moat, and other things necessary for defence." Meanwhile he had married a wealthy lady named Charlotte d'Argouges, and possibly had found her money useful in carrying out these warlike additions to his château, which, as a matter of fact, could very well have done without them, since it was never to be attacked. Not that Philippe du Moulin was not a fighter, for, like every gentleman of his day, he was a soldier by profession. But he used his energies in the service of his King and against no one save the enemies of his country. In his youth, in 1447, he had doubtless assisted Charles of Orleans in his fruitless attempt to conquer the Duchy of Milan, and after his marriage he had once more, under the leadership of Charles VIII, taken the road to Italy. The latter campaign had marked one of the turning-points in his life. Two months before the battle of Fornovo, in which, on July 6, 1495, some nine

thousand Frenchmen put to flight thirty-five
thousand Italians, he had been made a member
of the King's Council; a few hours before
the engagement, which had most far-reaching
effects on the world's history, he had been
knighted; and he had taken so prominent
a part in the fight as to merit special mention
by the chronicler, Philippe de Commynes.
Another historian, Jean de Serres, mentioned
him as one of a group of gentlemen who
had saved the King's life by coming to his
assistance when he had imprudently entered
a particularly dangerous part of the battle,
but Commynes, who had been an eye-witness,
gave a somewhat different and probably
correcter version. The author of *La Chronique
de Charles VIII* stated that the Bastard of
Bourbon and Philippe du Moulin had called
out to the King " Passez, Sire, passez ! " and
had thus made him take a place, mounted on
his famous one-eyed black charger Savoy, at
the head of the fight, in front of the standard.
As a result of this service more honours had
been heaped upon the builder of the Château
du Moulin; he had been made Captain of
Blaye and Governor of Langres, and,
generally speaking, had attained a high
position at Court. Had he not been the

King's Chamberlain, and in that quality one
of the pall-bearers at the funeral of Charles
VIII? Eight years later, on September 12,
1506, he himself had died at Langres,
regretting as the end drew near that he was
not in his beloved manor-house in the Sologne,
and expressing a wish, which was faithfully carried out, that his heart be placed in
the church he had built at Lassay. How a
simple fact like that brought one into touch
with the personality of this feudal knight!
Legend represented him to have been a miser,
but such a tender detail as that proved he
possessed sensibilities which are not usually
associated with avarice. The story ran that
he sought to hide a treasure beneath his
castle, and that the workman whom he
employed to make a hiding-place was led
there at dead of night and blindfolded, in
order that he might not know where he
was working. But at the conclusion of the
work Philippe du Moulin perceived that his
precautions were useless, so, drawing his
sword in a fit of anger, he killed the man
on the very spot where his gold was to be
hidden. A short time afterwards he was
stricken with remorse, and obtained the
Pope's absolution on the condition that he

built seven chapels, more than four of which
the superstitious inhabitants of the Sologne—
a district of legends—can still point out in
support of a story which, recalled even
under such favourable conditions as a moon-
light night, far from convinced me of its
truth.

Our visit to the château on the following
morning considerably added to my knowledge
of its history. It is built principally of red
and black bricks, so arranged as to form a
pleasing pattern of lozenges. It has neither
been added to nor undergone many alterations
since the fifteenth century, the only important
changes having been the destruction of some
of the towers of the fortress, the cutting down
of its walls to a convenient level, and the
removal of the drawbridge. A stone bridge
now leads over the moat to the *château-fort*,
the entrance of which is machicolated and
flanked by towers. Over the gateway, carved
on a block of stone, are the arms of Philippe
du Moulin: azure, three fesses argent, accompanied by two lions, surrounded by Renaissance ornamentation, as supporters. On the
door itself is the inscription: A DEO ET
VICTRICIB ARM—" A Deo et victricibus armis,"
which, in all likelihood, alludes to the Italian

campaign of Charles VIII, and is an acknowledg-
ment by Philip of the assistance he received
from God when fighting at Fornovo. His
arms are also to be seen on the mantelpiece
of one of the rooms situated above the entrance.
We found that the most interesting room in
this portion of the château was a kitchen with
beautiful vaulted roof. It has a broad deep
fireplace, and, in addition to a pair of fifteenth
century andirons, bearing the arms of Philippe
du Moulin, still possesses the roasting-wheel
which in feudal times was worked by
dogs.

The manor-house, which is detached from
the *château-fort*, consists of six large rooms
and a like number of smaller ones, with attics
and cellars. The principal room is that now
called the drawing-room, which is noteworthy
on account of its ceiling painted with a floral
design dating from the time of Francis I, its
curious prism-shaped main beam, and its
ancient windows. The chimney-piece, on
which are the arms of the various families to
whom the château has belonged, is modern
work, as is the case, indeed, with mantelpieces in other rooms. The original ones
were destroyed during the Revolution.

Adjoining this residence and communicating

THE DRAWING-ROOM AT THE CHÂTEAU DU MOULIN

THE MEDIÆVAL KITCHEN AT THE CHÂTEAU DU MOULIN

with the salon is a charming little chapel dating
from a period a little later than that of the
manor-house itself, and surmounted by a lead
cross of remarkable workmanship. The most
important thing it contains is a small primitive
statue of St. Catherine in painted stone,
probably one of a number of similar statues
which ornamented the chapel of the Moulin
family in the church at Lassay. One is led
to this conclusion by the fact that there are
certain empty brackets above the tomb in
which the heart of Philippe du Moulin is
enclosed, and because of the discovery at the
time of the restoration of the château of the
remains of another statue whose place can likewise be indicated in the parish church. "This
statue," says M. Paul Vitry, "is certainly
anterior to the construction of this charming
habitation . . . ; it may have been executed
during the first half of the fifteenth century.
It is a purely French work, without heaviness
of style or superabundance of detail. Its
drapery, which shows great skill and judgment,
and which at the same time is most simple,
has the same long, straight folds as the Virgin
of Marturet. Its fresh and youthful face
possesses the same quiet and penetrating grace,
with greater exuberance of health and less

5

roguishness than was found in the fourteenth
century, but without attaining, however, the
Flemish or Burgundian rotundity of the
fifteenth." And the same writer adds in a
note: "It is thus to be clearly distinguished
from other works equally charming, but in
which the Flemish character is more ac-
centuated; for instance, from another St.
Catherine which is in the Bulliot Collection
at Autun." [1]

There is an inscription on the right hand
side of the door of the chapel which reminds
me that I have so far mentioned but one
owner of the Château du Moulin. It records
the death, on April 3, 1563, of Jehan III, the
son and heir of Philippe du Moulin. He
married a lady named Gabrielle de La Chastre,
but as he had no children the château became
the property of his sister Margaret and her
husband Vincent du Puy. It was then owned
in succession by the allied houses of Anlezy,
Barbançon, Savare, and De Thuet, thus passing
from one descendant to another of Philippe
du Moulin for more than four centuries!
Only in 1902, in fact, was the chain broken
by its sale to the late M. Marcel de Marchéville, the father of the present owner, M. Louis

[1] *Michel Colombe et la Sculpture Française de son temps.*

de Marchéville. It was the former gentleman
who, with the assistance of M. Charles Génuys,
a well-known architect, undertook the restoration of the château,—a work which has been
accomplished with exemplary judgment and
skill. But one instance of the care which has
been taken need be given. Crowning the roof
of the *château-fort* is an elegant campanile
which until recent years was missing. The
existence of such a bell-tower was first brought
to light on closely examining a picture of the
château depicted in the background of a
curious fifteenth century fresco in the Du
Moulin chapel at the Lassay church; and
on a search being made for the site of
this tower it was at once discovered. Not
often is the restoration of an ancient building
aided in such an unexpected and interesting
manner.

A pilgrimage to this chapel to see the fresco
and the tomb of Philippe du Moulin was a
fitting conclusion to our visit to Lassay. The
picture represents St. Christopher crossing a
river with the infant Jesus on his shoulders;
in his left hand he holds a tree; and his
features are believed to be those of the knight
whose heart reposes in the tomb beneath the
painting. The stone statue of Philip, reclin-

ing on the tomb, is much damaged, but enough remains to show that his hands are joined in prayer, that his helmet and buckler are at his side, and that his feet are resting on a couchant lion.

CHAPTER III

BACK TO THE LOIRE: AT CHAUMONT AND AMBOISE

TO travel from the source to the mouth of an important river, and to note its varying characteristics as it grows in size and strength, must be counted among a traveller's most delightful experiences, whether he be a geographer, a moralist, or a mere dilettante. For, of all the inanimate things of Nature, a stream possesses the greatest semblance of humanity; it shares with its living associates the trees the honour of having a personality; and it is endowed with that quality of unobtrusive sociability which is ever found in the best companions. So, at least, we were pleased to think as, in a fanciful mood, we turned our backs on Blois and entered on the first stage of our journey down the Loire. Our plan was to follow for eighty miles the verdant valley through which it winds towards the sea, and we were naturally looking forward

to several days' intimate acquaintanceship with
a stream whose beauties form one of the
chief attractions of the scenery of Touraine.
Stretching out to distant horizons, bounded by
wooded slopes, the sandy-bedded river, with
its pollard willows and its green islets, adds
the necessary touch of animation to landscapes
which, characterised by that peaceful and
smiling picturesqueness which some one, centuries ago, summed up in the now hackneyed
phrase "The Garden of France," would
otherwise border on monotony.   It is the river
which gives this valley of green pastures and
cornfields and vine-clad ridges that note of
individuality which remains firmly fixed in the
memory long years after it has been visited.

Apart from these impressions, my notebook
contains little else than a bare record of our
ten-mile run to Chaumont.   The day, I see,
was bright and sunny.   A fresh breeze was
blowing from the sea, bringing with it the
scent of flowers and covering the scant waters
of the river, which flashed in the sunlight for
miles, with myriads of little waves.   Hundreds
of multi-coloured butterflies flitted and skipped
along the highway, prompting the remark
that Touraine must be one of the entomolo-
gist's ideal hunting-grounds.   And workers in

CHAUMONT

the fields, in attitudes reminiscent of figures in Millet's pictures, were cutting the corn—disdainful of modern machinery—with scythes and sickles. Amidst these surroundings did we finally come within sight of the heavy towers of the Château of Chaumont rising from the trees on a wooded ridge which skirts the left bank of the Loire.

Crossing the river by a creaking, swaying suspension bridge, we passed through the village, the houses of which run parallel with the water, and reached the entrance to the castle grounds. A long, steep, shady avenue, which mounts the hill until you are high above the spire of the village church, leads direct to the château, a formidable-looking building with stubborn machicolated towers and a drawbridge. Its architecture is a mixture of late Gothic and early Renaissance. Sparingly ornamented, its embellishments are yet sufficiently striking to arrest the attention. Above the porch are the crowned initials of Louis XII and Anne of Brittany, surrounded by fleurs-de-lis; on the right and left towers are the arms of Charles of Chaumont and those of his famous brother Cardinal George of Amboise; whilst on both appear the interlaced initials and the flaming mountain which

the former nobleman, who was Grand Master
of France under Louis XII, and the builder of
the château, chose as his emblems.   On other
parts of the towers can also be seen the initials
of Henry II and Catherine de' Medici, but
these, like those of Louis and Anne, were
placed there merely as symbols of allegiance,
and are not an indication that it was a royal
residence.   Their interest, therefore, is secondary to that which we feel for the arms and
initials of the two men whose names recall the
early history of this celebrated castle.

George of Amboise was born in 1460 in a
château which preceded the present one, and
which had belonged to his family since the
twelfth century.   The history of this earlier
fortress can be traced even farther back than
that,—as far back, indeed, as the end of the
tenth century, when Eudes I, Count of Blois,
one of Theobald the Trickster's successors,
recognised the strategic importance of this point
of the valley of the Loire.   It is unnecessary,
however, to do more than mention this primitive stronghold, seeing that one's interest
nowadays is almost wholly centred on the
existing château and on the various families to
whom it has belonged.

Passing from one member of the Amboise

family to another, it came into the possession, about the middle of the sixteenth century, of Charles and Antoine de la Rochefoucauld, the sons of Antoinette of Amboise, the great-great-niece of the builder of the château. But they did not long retain it, owing to its purchase in 1560 by Catherine de' Medici, who required it for a somewhat curious purpose. In the previous year, the accession to the throne of Francis II had been marked by bitter rivalry between Catherine and Diana of Poitiers, who, in addition to being exiled from Court, had been made to return the Crown jewels. Now, among the gifts which the fair favourite had received from Henry II was the Château of Chenonceaux, — the one country mansion above all others which Catherine had the greatest desire to possess. So she determined, by fair means or foul, to obtain it. A threat to revoke all the gifts of Francis I and Henry II brought Diana to terms : she agreed to exchange Chenonceaux for Chaumont. Up to this point history is perfectly clear. However, one important question remains to be considered :—Was Chaumont in Catherine's possession for a number of years before the transaction, as has been contended, or did she buy it simply with the object of an exchange ?

Unfortunately for all the fine romantic stories which have been built up around Catherine and Chaumont, not to mention the brilliant work of misguided restorers, of which more anon, it would seem that the latter hypothesis must be accepted as the correct one. For an unbroken list of owners of the château can be shown for the years during which she is said to have owned it, and, moreover, the exact date on which she became the legal owner is now known,—March 21, 1560,—although, strange to say, the exchange of châteaux took place on the previous January 4.

Without entering into the respective merits of Chaumont and Chenonceaux, subsequent events show that Diana had by no means the best of the bargain. She did not come into possession of her new home until April 27. But even then she could hardly call it her own ; and it was not, in fact, until April 9, 1562, that she was left to enjoy it at her ease. Four years later she died, leaving her property to her daughter, the Duchess of Bouillon.

Coming down to the eighteenth century, Chaumont was sold in 1739 to Nicolas Bertin de Vaugien, who destroyed a façade facing the Loire and made other architectural alterations. Eleven years later, under a new owner, Jacques

Donatien Le Ray, its fortunes underwent a
startling change : it became the scene of
industrial activity, one form of which was a
manufactory of terra-cotta medallions designed
and executed by an Italian artist Jean Baptiste
Nini, whose works are now much sought after
by collectors.   M. Le Ray was a generous-
hearted, broad-minded gentleman, and a daring
man of business to boot.   He was a friend of
Franklin, who, whilst acting as American
Minister to France from 1777 to 1785, lived
rent-free in one of his houses adjoining the
Hôtel de Valentinois, at Passy, in the suburbs
of Paris.   During the first year of his residence
in the capital Franklin was, in all probability,
a guest at Chaumont, for one of Nini's finest
works is a portrait-medallion of the great
envoy, dated 1777.   M. Le Ray devoted a
large part of his fortune to colonisation
schemes in the United States.   On his death
in 1803 these were continued by his eldest
son, who regarded that country as so much
his own as to fight for her in the War of
Independence.   Whilst he was still in America,
Madame de Staël, another of the friends of
this liberty-loving father and son, had one
of her numerous quarrels with Napoleon, and
was exiled from Paris ; so M. Le Ray *fils*

gallantly placed Chaumont at her disposal.
On his return to France in 1823 he sold the
château to Baron d'Etchégoyen. Ten years
afterwards it became the property of Count
and Countess Sauvan d'Aramon, who, seeing
that it was falling into ruins, began its restoration. This work, which was carried out
by M. de la Morandière, an architect of
the school of Félix Duban, under whom
he worked at the Château of Blois, was
continued by Viscount Walsh, the Countess'
second husband. The death of Viscountess
Walsh in 1872 brings us to the time when
the château was sold to Mlle. Say, who, a few
months after purchasing it, married Prince
Henri Amédée de Broglie, the great-grandson
of the authoress of *Corinne*. The Prince and
Princess, who are still the owners of the
château, continued its restoration until quite
recently, and, as we found on visiting the
interior, have beautified its rooms with many
fine pieces of furniture and works of art
dating from the fifteenth, sixteenth, and
seventeenth centuries.

Conscious of that feeling of respect with
which every building of renown should be
approached, and especially when entrance is
being sought to one that is a private residence,

ENTRANCE TO THE CHÂTEAU OF CHAUMONT

CHAUMONT: A PORTION OF THE COURTYARD

we rang a bell at the postern. We were admitted immediately and shown into a large courtyard, one side of which is open to the valley. The view from this quadrilateral platform is magnificent,—the eye can follow the river, both up and down its winding course, for mile upon mile, until, at last, it becomes but a mere silver thread in the distance. Well content were we to be left there, before seeing the historical rooms of the château, to enjoy it at our ease, and also to examine the courtyard in detail. Richer in ornamentation than the exterior of the castle, it contains several things worthy of note, such as a carved stone well with beautifully proportioned wrought-iron super-structure, a small Renaissance doorway, a painted corridor composed of arcades with sculptured capitals, and the carvings on the outer pillars of the Louis XII staircase leading to the first storey of the right wing of the château—the only storey, by the bye, which is open to the public.

It is evident that much time and thought, assisted by a long purse, have been spent over the decoration and furnishing of Chaumont, and, on the whole, with satisfactory results. If errors have been committed, I must at the

same time admit that they do not seriously
interfere with the picture of the past which
its rooms and their contents call before the
mind.   The rather diminutive guardroom
is appropriately ornamented with fifteenth
and sixteenth century arms and armour ; in
its wide fireplace stand huge bronze andirons ;
beautiful old furniture is on every side ; on
its walls are choice Flemish paintings and
Beauvais tapestries ; and its painted ceiling,
dating from the middle of the sixteenth century,
bears the arms of the Houses of Chaumont
and Amboise.   We noticed but one jarring
note in this eminently fine room—and that
could easily be remedied.   I refer to some
show-cases containing *souvenirs de Chaumont*—
cheap jewellery and crudely coloured pottery,
placed there by the *concierge* to tempt the
inartistic visitor, and in such close proximity
to rare works of art, including a fine Italian
seat with a back in *gêsso* work, as positively
to shock a connoisseur's nerves.   Surely these
trumpery objects should be relegated to their
proper sphere—the janitor's lodge ?   In an
adjoining room, called the Council Chamber,
our attention was attracted first by a magnificent tiled floor brought from Palermo, representing a hunting scene, and secondly by some

specimens of Italian faience. But these did
not long retain us, anxious as we were to
reach the so-called bedroom of Catherine de'
Medici and that of Ruggieri, her astrologer.
Infinite care has been taken to furnish the
former with as many relics of the Queen as could
be obtained : her bed, her toilet-table, her
praying-desk, and even her *corbeille de mariage*.
As historical curiosities these are undoubtedly
full of interest. But how misleading they are
when set out in a room bearing the name of
the great Florentine, and how open to criticism
is the work of those restorers who have gone
to legend rather than to history for their
inspiration ! Naturally, the conclusion arrived
at by a person unacquainted with the facts is
that Chaumont was once the Queen's residence,
the scene of her extraordinary political activity,
and of her astrological studies. Ruggieri's
room, the mantelpiece of which is ornamented
with cabalistic signs, and which, it is said,
communicates with an observatory by means
of a secret staircase, is contiguous and confirms
the impression. Yet nothing is farther from
the truth. As I have already shown, Catherine
was never anything save a nominal owner
of the château, which she bought merely
in order to exchange it for another. There

is not a tittle of historical evidence in her
correspondence to show that she ever resided
there.   In fact, the only basis for the conten-
tion that she was intimately connected with
Chaumont is the legend recorded by Nicolas
Pasquier in 1610, and repeated by Félibien in
1680, that Ruggieri revealed to her at this
castle the number of years her children and
their successors would reign.   Admitting that
there may be a grain of truth in this story,
and that during the reign of Henry II
Catherine and the Court made occasional visits
to Chaumont, as they were accustomed to do
to various châteaux, it is, at any rate, certain
that the room in which her astrological *séances*
were held no longer exists.   For we are told
that it formed part of the " oldest buildings "
and had " a view of the water," from which
it is evident that it was situated in the wing
destroyed in the eighteenth century.   Con-
fronted with these disillusionising facts, both
Catherine's and Ruggieri's room will be found
to be the least satisfactory of the historical
apartments of Chaumont, though they are
intended to be the most important.   Had the
bed and the other objects which belonged to
her been in the northern wing of the Château
of Blois their effect would have been magnifi-

cent; as it is, you look upon them with very
little more emotion than if they had been in
an ordinary museum. A fine collection of
Nini's medallions in the same room is much
more in its place. The bedroom which is
said to have been that occupied by Diana of
Poitiers has also, I suspect, been arbitrarily
chosen. It is situated in one of the towers,
is exceedingly modest in size, and its only
entrance is from the guardroom, where the clash
of arms and the boisterous laughter of the
soldiery can hardly have contributed to the rest
of the fair occupant of the adjoining chamber.

To wander in the delightful park which
surrounds the Château of Chaumont was a
pleasure denied to us, warned as we were by
a notice-board that to stray from the main
avenue was forbidden, so as there was nothing
more to be seen we left the sleepy little village
and, still descending the Loire, proceeded to
Amboise, which held forth attractions second
to none save those of Blois itself. For
Amboise, owing to its situation at the confluent of the Loire and the Masse, is one of
the oldest towns in Touraine, and possesses a
castle whose story is interwoven with the
history of France. The Gauls were the first
to recognise how well the plateau at the

6

junction of the two rivers commanded the
valley of the Loire ; the Romans, too, were
quick to see its suitability for an encampment ;
and the Counts of Anjou built there a Gothic
château which existed until as late as the end
of the fifteenth century. It was on the site
of this early building, in which but one
noteworthy event took place, the interview
between Thomas à Becket and Louis VII, who
had undertaken to bring about a reconciliation between the Archbishop and Henry II of
England, that the present castle was built by
Charles VIII and his successors. The work
was begun about 1490, but it was not completed until the reign of Francis I.

The afternoon was still young when we
obtained our first glimpse of Amboise, and as
we approached by way of the two bridges
over the Loire, which at this point of the
river is divided into two branches by the Ile
St. Jean, we imagined we had chanced on the
ideal hour for seeing it. But, in our enthusiasm at finding so royal and imposing a
building, we were mistaken. The best time
for viewing it is towards evening, when the
shadows cast by the stooks in the cornfields
and by the poplars along the roadside are
growing longer and longer, and when the last

AMBOISE

rays of the declining sun light up its massive
towers and its pinnacled windows. Then,
enclosed to right and left in a mass of
greenery, does it stand out in greatest relief,
its white stonework turned to gold and its
ornamentation enhanced a hundredfold by
virtue of the coloured glow of evening.
Standing on an elevated tongue of land, it
towers above the distinctly dusty little town,
the ancient houses of which run alongside the
river and cluster beneath its precipitous walls.
These have such an air of impregnability that
we failed at first to discover a means of reaching the summit of the plateau, and it was only
on attacking them in the rear that we espied
the entrance, a simple opening in a low wall,
guarded by nothing more redoubtable than
two decrepit mendicants. From this point
can be obtained a good view of the exterior of
St. Hubert's Chapel, an exquisite construction
with a slender, graceful spire encircled by
gilded antlers. Ascending a winding path
and passing through a lofty tunnel cut in the
hillside, we at last reached the castle grounds,
where the first thing to be seen was the
entrance and interior of this chapel, which
was built by Charles VIII partly before and
partly after his Italian campaign.

Commynes relates that the young King
brought back with him from Naples several
excellent Italian artists and workmen, and that
in whatever country he saw beautiful things—
whether in France, in Italy, or in Flanders—
he secured them.   Among these Italian artists
were Guido Pagaganino, a " maker of images,"
and his wife and daughter, both of whom were
painters.   They and their compatriots were
exclusively employed on the interior decoration
of the château, as is clear from the fact that
its architecture bears no trace of Italian
influence.   Similarly, the general style of
St. Hubert's Chapel is undoubtedly French.
Only on examining its ornamentation can
a foreign element be detected, the delicate
sculpture of the interior and the work in high
relief over the doorway (I do not refer, of
course, to the figures of Charles and Anne of
Brittany kneeling to the Virgin, which are
quite modern) having been executed either by
Flemish sculptors or copied from Flemish
models by French workmen.   This beautiful
alto-rilievo represents the vision of St. Hubert.
The famous huntsman, who, according to
legend, was converted one fête day whilst
hunting in the Forest of Ardennes, and who
afterwards became Bishop of Liège, is to be

ST. HUBERT'S CHAPEL AT AMBOISE AND ENTRANCE TO THE CASTLE

ENTRANCE TO ST. HUBERT'S CHAPEL AT AMBOISE

seen to the right with his horse and dogs;
and the sculptor has represented him in the
act of kneeling on one knee before the miraculous stag between whose antlers, as he hears
a voice crying "Hubert! Hubert! how long
wilt thou spend thy time uselessly? Knowest
thou not that thou wert born to know, to love,
and to serve thy Creator?" there springs forth
a crucifix. To the left are two other figures:
one St. Christopher bearing Christ on his
shoulders and resting on a long stick, and the
other a monk standing at the door of a chapel
with something in his hand resembling a
lantern, as though he were guiding the saint
across a river. By the bye, there is another
piece of sculpture at Amboise which is likewise characteristically Flemish and which
supports the belief that Charles really did draw
upon Flanders when embellishing his castle; it
is a high relief representing a mounted knight
giving alms to a poor man, and we saw it on
a house side before crossing the Loire. Its
family likeness to the Vision of St. Hubert is
too striking to be merely a coincidence.

St. Hubert's Chapel, the buildings facing
the Loire, and the famous towers which are
provided with inclined planes instead of staircases, so gentle in their slope that carriages

can mount to the top without difficulty, were Charles' contribution to Amboise. He did not live to see the completion of the château. On April 7, 1498, whilst watching a game of tennis, he was struck down by apoplexy and died almost immediately.[1] Louis XII continued for five years to carry out his plans. And Francis, who, having spent part of his youth at Amboise, continued to live there during the early years of his reign, made such further additions to the castle as were needed to bring it practically to a finished state. At the beginning of 1516 he also had a little manor-house, situated not far from the castle and known as the Château de Cloux, put into thorough repair, ready for the arrival of Leonardo da Vinci, who, at the age of over sixty, had consented to leave his native country and place his genius as painter, engineer, and architect at the King's service. Leonardo, whom Francis allowed a salary of 700 écus, about £1400, was accompanied by a favourite pupil Francesco da Melzi. He had been in declining health (though his spirits were still those of a young man) for some time before

[1] The story of him having met his death by striking his head against the lintel of a doorway ornamented with a porcupine is incorrect.

leaving Italy, and he lived but three years
after his arrival at Amboise. As the end drew
near, his right hand became paralysed, so, on
April 23, 1519, a week before his death, he
summoned a notary, Maître Boreau, to the
little house which he was accustomed to call
a palace, and dictated his will. Although the
practice of this Amboise lawyer was handed
down from father to son until as late as 1885,
Leonardo's original will was found to have
disappeared from the notarial archives. Fortunately an authentic copy of the Italian text
of this precious document, dating from the
seventeenth century, was discovered some years
ago. Among the painter's last requests were
minute directions for his burial in the royal
church of St. Florentin, which, prior to 1808,
the date of its destruction, stood in the grounds
of the Château of Amboise. He was accordingly buried in the cloisters, but exactly where
is now unknown. Arsène Houssaye, one of
the most prolific of French writers, claimed to
have discovered the spot in 1863, when he
made excavations on the site of the church,
and even to have identified Leonardo's skull
among a number of bones which were
brought to light ; but there can be no doubt
that he was mistaken, seeing that Vinci was

interred, as I have said, in the cloisters and
not in the church itself. However, the poet
and novelist was considered to have established
a case strong enough to warrant the erection
of a bust of Leonardo on the place where the
remains were found, and these, enclosed in a
lead box, were buried under the flagstones in
St. Hubert's Chapel.

Before leaving Amboise we naturally did
not fail to walk up the Rue Victor Hugo,
and a few yards along the Rue du Clos-Lucé,
to see the great painter's house, a pretty construction in red brick and stone which now
bears the name of the Château of Clos-Lucé,
and which, having undergone careful restoration, has much the appearance that it had in
the days of Francis. Being a private residence,
inexorably closed to the public, we did not
visit its interior, which, however, would have
had little interest for us, since, as I understand,
it has undergone such changes as make it
difficult to point out the room in which
Leonardo passed away in the presence of his
three devoted friends Melzi, Villaris, and
Salaï. Vasari states that he died in King
Francis' arms, but that is a legend which
modern historians have long since shown
to be without foundation.

After the reign of Francis I, with its
pleasant memories of Leonardo da Vinci, the
Château of Amboise became the scene of one
of those grim tragedies which have so often
darkened the history of France. In 1560,
under Francis II, a number of Huguenots
and Catholics, who were discontented with
the growing influence of the House of Guise,
formed a conspiracy there with the object of
seizing the Duke of Guise and his brother,
and of removing the King from their power.
The conspirators, whose leaders were the
Prince of Condé and a nobleman of Périgord
named La Renaudie, planned to get possession
of the castle during the dinner-hour; and they
would most probably have succeeded but for
the treachery of one of their number, a Paris
advocate named d'Avenelles. To avert the
danger, the Duke of Guise hid his troops in
the forest and attacked the conspirators as
they approached the château in small detach-
ments. A large number of them were killed;
the others were captured to a man and reserved, without even a pretence of a trial, for
the cruellest of tortures. Some were broken
on the wheel; others were hanged from the
castle windows and from the iron balcony
facing the Loire; and others, again, were

drowned in the river. The most privileged among them were beheaded. And, whilst these daily massacres were in progress, the members of the House of Guise regarded them as a fitting after-dinner spectacle for the ladies, who, according to Régnier de la Planche, looked on from the windows of the château with apparently as little emotion as though they had been at the play.

As in the case of the Château of Blois after the murder of the Duke of Guise and the Cardinal of Lorraine, these tragic events were the signal, as it were, for the decadence of the Château of Amboise. Henceforth it ceased to play any important part in history. In the seventeenth century it was degraded to the level of a State prison, the most illustrious man to be enclosed within its walls being Nicolas Foucquet, that dishonest Superintendent of Finance of Louis xiv who, with his peculated millions, built the magnificent Château of Vaux, near Melun. In 1760 it became the property of the Duke of Choiseul ; on his death it was bought by the Crown and resold for five million francs to the Duke of Penthièvre ; and from his family it passed into the hands of that of Orleans. Confiscated by the French Govern-

AMBOISE: THE CASTLE COURTYARD AND GARDEN

THE MONUMENT TO LEONARDO DA VINCI AT AMBOISE

ment, it was again used as a prison, this time for Abd-el-Kader, the brave emir who offered such a stubborn resistance to the French in Algeria, and who, on being set free by Louis Napoleon on condition of his not returning to his native country, showed that he could keep his word better than his captors had done in 1847, when he was promised that if he surrendered he should be allowed to retire to Alexandria or St. Jean d'Acre. By means of a Bill passed in 1872, the Château of Amboise was restored to the House of Orleans, which, still possessing it, has turned it into an alms-house for the superannuated servants of the various branches of the family.

Of all the royal residences of the Loire no château has undergone so much mutilation as Amboise. The restoration of its exterior has, therefore, been the work of many years, and is, indeed, even now still far from complete. As regards its interior, the rooms have, of course, long since lost the decorations with which they were beautified by Charles' Italian artists ; and, since the task of restoring them to anything like their original appearance has been recognised as vain, they contain nothing worthy of special note. The beauties of Amboise are, in fact, purely external ones.

One thing in particular made us envy those old retainers who have found a home—and a right pleasant one it must be!—within its walls : the castle garden and grounds, which, at the height of summer, are resplendent with colour and abound with the most delightful shady spots.   Near the monument to Leonardo da Vinci is a quincunx of lime trees under which we had a strong desire to linger.   The branches are trained so as to meet at the top and form a roof of tender green, through which the sunlight, charging the atmosphere with colour, filtered in that subtle manner which the most skilful painters have sometimes had a difficulty in rendering, and, streaming through the leaves, formed a pattern on the ground of verdant light and shadow.   However, the regret we felt on leaving this little avenue was soon effaced, for a few minutes later we were gazing on the view of the valley of the Loire from the battlements of the Tour des Minimes,—a view similar to that at Chaumont, and which, when seen by La Fontaine, drew from him the declaration that it was the most smiling and varied landscape he had ever looked upon.

CHAPTER IV

AT TOURS: DELICACIES AND DIVAGATIONS

THOUGH it may be true that quite a number of French provincial towns can justly boast of their superiority, in certain respects, to Tours, I hold that none can lay claim to such an aggregation of virtues as the ancient capital of Touraine. Yet, numerous and varied as its attractions are, they are not immediately apparent to the passing visitor; and it was not until we had resided for some weeks within a short distance of this pleasant town, and had seen into how many categories it is possible to divide those who go there with specific objects in view, that we began to discover and appreciate all its good qualities. Take, for instance, the traveller, who represents the most important class of visitor, and whose principal desire is to see beautiful old buildings. Where will he find a town which has attained such a world-wide reputation as Tours, which,

as one of the oldest towns in France, has both
numerous ancient constructions and a most
interesting history ? It is no less renowned,
too, in the eyes of the epicure, to whom its
name has become a synonym for certain tooth-
some viands called *rillettes* and *rillons*, which
Balzac, who was a native of Tours,—he was
born at 39 Rue Nationale, and his statue faces
the Place du Palais-de-Justice, — describes
in *Le Lys dans la Vallée* as " that brown
preserve . . . that preparation so much
esteemed by some *gourmets*," and as " that
residuum of pork fried in its own fat and
resembling cooked truffles." I once had
occasion to hear a *gourmet*—he was also, let
me add, a *vieil enfant de la Touraine*, which to
a certain extent explains his enthusiasm—
discourse for half an hour on the merits of
this kind of potted meat and these brown
nodules of ham ; and he assured me, in concluding, that no dinner could be accounted
complete unless it were preceded by one or
other of these delicacies, and was washed down
by the celebrated effervescing white wine of
Vouvray, a village a few miles from Tours.
Every bit as deep as the affection of the
gastronome, though inspired by different
considerations, is that of the English or

American mother with a daughter whose education requires the finishing touches putting to it. Tours and the suburbs are noted for their schools and *pensions*, where young ladies can acquire quite as pure French as is spoken in Paris,—and under infinitely healthier conditions. Easily distinguished by their dress and accent, they can be seen at all times of the year, under the care of a chaperone, gazing into the shop-windows or sitting in the tea-rooms of the animated Rue Nationale. During the summer and towards the hour of five o'clock, you will also frequently see in those much patronised afternoon resorts the Parisian lady of fashion, who knows that she can count on finding in Tours a less harassing round of social pleasures than she has had in the capital, and at the same time just as good society. Somewhat similarly, the man of business (by no means the last of those who turn their eyes longingly in the direction of this provincial town) jumps into his autocar and hastens there to escape for a spell from the stress of city life. Even the child has a good word to say for Tours, its barley-sugar, and its prunes.

We could not have hit on more delightful quarters: a vine-covered cottage in a district

of vineyards and orchards, on a hill above the
Cher, which, as it approaches Tours from
Bléré, flows into the valley of the Loire and
soon joins its sister river.   Behind the house
was our garden, scented with many roses,
ablaze with geraniums, shaded by fruit trees,
and under the lee of a pine wood, whence,
especially towards evening, a faint resinous
odour was wafted on the breeze.   There, in
the sweet pure air, we took our meals, not
forgetting to see that our table was furnished
with the delicacies of Tours ; there we read
Balzac and rested from the fatigue of our
recent journeys.

It is the duty of every one who travels in
Touraine to renew acquaintance with certain
of the stories of the great novelist.   They
have an added interest when read amidst the
natural beauties among which they were
conceived and, in some cases, I believe,
written ; even though the writer's descriptions
of those beauties are not particularly striking,
and his references to châteaux and localities be
of little practical value.   To follow once more
the love story of Félix and Mme. de Mortsauf
in *Le Lys dans la Vallée*, to sympathise afresh
with the Abbé Birotteau in *Le Curé de
Tours*, and to laugh for the hundredth time

over *Les Contes Drolatiques* is a most excellent
method of putting you in tune with your
surroundings. Though we got but slight
topographical or historical information from
these books, there was one noteworthy fact
we gathered from one of them,—that Tours
in Balzac's time must have been rather
intellectually dull, and in other ways very
different from the active, progressive town it is
to-day. " It was then," he says, " one of the
least literary towns in France ; " whereas it
is now an important centre for literary and
antiquarian research, as witness one only of
its learned societies, the Société Archéologique
de la Touraine, the transactions of which are
of the greatest value to those who are studying
the history of the ancient province. As to its
modern buildings, the one in which its inhabitants of seventy years ago apparently took
the most pride was the bridge over the Loire,
which Balzac calls " one of the finest monuments of French architecture." If you were
to ask a Tourangeau of to-day to indicate
the finest modern construction in his native
town, this bridge would be the last thing he
would think of ; he would, in all probability,
point out the new Hôtel de Ville, or the
new basilica of Saint Martin, both imposing

7

buildings due to Laloux, an architect who is held in much honour for the double reason that he is a man of talent and a child of Tours.

Good, however, as the modern buildings are, the ancient ones far exceed them in interest, and on the occasions on which we dragged ourselves from our rose-garden on the hill our attention was devoted almost exclusively to the latter. Of these the most important is the Cathedral, dedicated to Saint Gatianus, the first Bishop of Tours, and built, on the ruins of a still older church, at various times between 1225 and 1547. The choir dates from the thirteenth, the transept from the fourteenth, and the nave from the fifteenth centuries. Its magnificent stained - glass windows, in a perfect state of preservation, also date from these centuries, according to their position, the finest being a series of fifteen in the topmost windows of the choir. The blues in these thirteenth century master-pieces are superbly rich, and give the impression rather of the colour of precious stones than that of glass. These windows and the white marble tomb of the children of Charles VIII and Anne of Brittany—a tomb fashioned in the Renaissance style, early in the sixteenth century, either by the brothers

TOURS CATHEDRAL

Juste or under the direction of Michel Colombe—are the finest things to be seen in the interior. The principal façade, with its three large flamboyant doors and its slightly dissimilar towers, surmounted by octagonal storeys dating from the Renaissance, will also be found to be well worth several minutes' thoughtful inspection from a point of vantage on the little square above which it towers so nobly. Prior to the Revolution there existed in Tours a still larger and finer religious edifice than the Cathedral: an immense basilica which was built in the twelfth and thirteenth centuries over the tomb of Saint Martin, whose body had been brought to Tours from Candès about the year 400. It was more than one hundred yards in length, over seventy yards in breadth, and nearly thirty yards in height. Like the celebrated Abbey of Cluny, in Paris, it was almost totally destroyed, early in the nineteenth century, to make way for a new street. The only portions remaining are two towers, the Tour de l'Horloge and the Tour Charlemagne, and a gallery of one of the cloisters, which can be seen in the courtyard of a religious establishment in the Rue Descartes. The towers, which have a most solitary appearance, rising from amidst

the houses, and which are so isolated that
it seems impossible that they ever belonged
to the same building, date, as I have said,
from the twelfth and thirteenth centuries ;
but the gallery of the cloister was built
between 1508 and 1519 by Bastien François,
the nephew of Michel Colombe.   There are
several other antiquated churches in Tours,
but old houses and ancient châteaux being the
principal object of our visit to Touraine, we
did no more than peep into Saint Julien,
Saint Saturnin, and Notre Dame la Riche,
though that is no reason why you should
follow our bad example.   In the neighbourhood of Saint Saturnin, and in the tangle of
narrow streets branching off from the Place
Plumereau, we found many examples of
fourteenth, fifteenth, and sixteenth century
houses, including a few with wooden fronts
ornamented with roughly carved, naive
statuettes.   One of the most celebrated is
a house of brick and stone in the Rue
Briçonnet, which goes by the name of the
House of Tristan l'Hermite, because some
ignorant person, possibly in the days of Balzac,
when he had not the opportunity of learning
better, mistook the tassled rope of Anne of
Brittany, with which a portion of the façade

"MAISON DE TRISTAN L'HERMITE" AT TOURS

is decorated, to be the emblem of Louis xi's hangsman! It was never, of course, in any way connected with that sinister Provost of the Marshals of France, and, indeed, was not built until the end of the fifteenth century, during the reign of Charles viii. A still older house—it was built in 1440—is the Hôtel Gouin at 35 Rue de Commerce, in the same quarter. Its almost pure white stone façade, facing a courtyard opening on the street, is one mass of lovely arabesques, which present so fresh an appearance, thanks to careful restoration, that you might almost imagine they were carved but yesterday. Seeing these two buildings in rapid succession, it is hard not to regret that they did not fall into the hands of equally thoughtful owners, for the "Maison de Tristan," unfortunately, is in as dilapidated a condition as the Hôtel Gouin is well-preserved. Near the Church of Saint Julien, in the Rue Saint François de Paule, stands a third fine old house, the Hôtel de Semblançay, so called because it was built by Jacques de Beaune, Baron of Semblançay, the treasurer to Francis i, who was accused, it is difficult to say whether rightly or wrongly, of malversation, and hanged at Montfaucon on August 12, 1527.

Going farther afield, we spent the best part
of one afternoon in visiting Plessis-les-Tours,
where Louis XI, in 1463, built a château, the
history of which has become inseparable from
his name.   But we met with a bitter disappointment there.   All that now remains of
the King's favourite residence is one wing in
red brick and stone, and the splendid park
which once surrounded it has been reduced to
the area of a small market-garden.   A meek,
soft-voiced person, who undertook to be our
guide, made a brave attempt to interest us in
things which, even when viewed with a good
deal of imagination, were incapable of creating
a spark of enthusiasm.   She led us to the
summit of a small winding staircase to show
us a view of a district which in no way
resembled a park where royal hunting parties
and royal interviews had once been held ; she
showed us a dismantled room in which Louis,
a victim of superstitious terrors, is said to
have given up his last breath ; she took us
into a so-called guardroom on the ground-
floor, restored to something like its ancient
appearance by the Tours doctor who owns
the château, and containing nothing more
interesting than some human bones found
whilst opening up the moat ; she pointed out

the cramped cell in the grounds where Cardinal La Balue, confined in one of Louis' celebrated iron cages, is supposed to have pined for years ; and she told us ineffectual stories of subterranean passages which, again according to legend, communicated with the House of Tristan l'Hermite !   I am afraid she must have found us singularly unappreciative ; but, really, it was impossible to feel even moderately excited over such a poor substitute for the picture we had formed of the Château of Plessis-les-Tours.   Had we had *Quentin Durward* with us I should have been inclined to have sat down, there and then, to read aloud certain passages of that stirring romance, in order to quicken our blood into its natural warmth, though I am fully aware that Scott's description of the castle is very exaggerated. "There were," he writes, "three external walls, battlemented and turreted from space to space, and at each angle, the second enclosure rising higher than the first, and being built so as to command the exterior defence in case it was won by the enemy ; and being again, in the same manner, itself commanded by the third and innermost barrier.   Around the external wall . . . was sunk a ditch of about twenty feet in depth. . . . In front of the second enclosure . . . there ran another fosse, and a third, both of the same unusual dimensions, was led between the second and the innermost enclosure. The verge, both of the outer and inner circuit of this triple moat, was strongly fenced with palisades of iron, serving the purpose of what are called *chevaux-de-frise* in modern fortification, the top of each pale being divided into a cluster of sharp spikes, which seemed to render any attempt to climb over an act of self-destruction. Far within the innermost enclosure arose the castle itself, containing buildings of different periods, crowded around, and united with the ancient and grim-looking donjon-keep, which was older than any of them, and which rose, like a black Ethiopian giant, high into the air, while the absence of any windows larger than shot-holes, irregularly disposed for defence, gave the spectator the same unpleasant feeling which we experience on looking at a blind man. The other buildings seemed scarcely better adapted for the purposes of comfort, for the windows opened to an inner and enclosed courtyard, so that the whole external front looked much more like that of a prison than a palace. The reigning king had even increased this effect; for, desirous that the

additions which he himself had made to the
fortifications should be of a character not
easily distinguished from the original building
(for, like many jealous persons, he loved not
that his suspicions should be observed), the
darkest-coloured brick and freestone were
employed, and soot mingled with the lime,
so as to give the whole castle the same
uniform tinge of extreme and rude antiquity."
And the novelist adds, a few pages farther on,
that the environs of the castle, with the
exception of a single winding path leading
to the portal, "were surrounded with every
species of hidden pitfall, snare, and gin, to
entrap the wretch who should venture thither
without a guide"; and that the victims of
Tristan l'Hermite were to be seen in the
neighbourhood "hanging like grapes from
every tree." Decidedly, the real Château of
Plessis did not deserve to be painted in such
black colours. One or two well-garnished
gibbets there may have been, and it is quite
possible that Louis protected certain parts of
his grounds with caltraps, as he did at the
Château des Forges, near Chinon; but the
rest, like much that has been related about
the King himself, is pure fiction. Francesco
Florio, a contemporary historian, states that

Louis chose Plessis-les-Tours as a site for his residence because of its picturesqueness, so it is hardly likely he would disfigure its beauty in the various manners related by Scott. Indeed, far from being the grim castle depicted in *Quentin Durward*, Plessis-les-Tours was a most agreeable manor-house, surrounded by a park so beautiful that it was called "The Garden of France" (a description afterwards extended to the whole of Touraine), and enjoying a view from its windows of the wooded slopes of Saint Cyr and Joué. "It is built," says Léon Godefroy, in an account of a visit which he made there in 1638, "principally of brick, except one side which is constructed entirely of freestone, and furnished with many windows. It is covered all over with fleurs-de-lis, mingled with ermines and porcupines and crowned characters." Not even so much as this remained of its decoration about the middle of the eighteenth century, and the buildings still standing were of so little architectural importance that, in 1773, they were used as a reformatory. The Revolution was the signal for a further step in the degeneration of a once famous castle; it was sold as national property, and whilst its buildings fell, little by little, into ruins, its park was slowly transformed into the present malodorous district of piggeries and unsightly cottages. Never did a royal domain meet with a more unworthy end.

When returning to Tours our attention was drawn, near the Botanical Gardens, to a farm called La Rabaterie, a fifteenth century building which is believed to have had a close connection with the Château of Plessis. It was the manor-house of Olivier le Daim, the barber-minister of Louis XI. Scott describes him as "a little, pale, meagre man, whose black silk jerkin and hose, without either coat, cloak, or cassock, formed a dress ill qualified to set off to advantage a very ordinary person. . . . His visage was penetrating and quick, although he endeavoured to banish such expression from his features, by keeping his eyes fixed on the ground, while, with the stealthy and quiet pace of a cat, he seemed modestly rather to glide than to walk through the apartment." La Rabaterie is not very remarkable in itself, but should curiosity or a sense of duty take you to Plessis-les-Tours you may as well see it, if only to enable you to recall the novelist's vivid portrayal of its former owner.

On our next excursion we met with better
fortune than that which attended our visit to
Plessis.   In fact, passing in review our various
divagations around Tours, my recollections of
the day spent at Vernou and the Château of
Jallanges are the pleasantest I have to recall,
partly, perhaps, because we passed so many
interesting places on the way.   The first was
Saint Symphorien, principally noteworthy for
the doorway of its sixteenth century church ;
then came the ruins of the Abbey of Mar-
moutier, founded by Saint Martin ; then the
Lantern of Rochecorbon, a curious observation
tower dating from the fourteenth century ;
and, finally, the village of Vouvray, the white
wine of which is held in repute by all epicures
from the simplest *bourgeois* of Tours to the
Czar of Russia.   But we did not allow its
temptations to detain us there more than a
quarter of an hour, anxious as we were to
push on to Vernou, which is situated a mile
or two farther on, in the valley of the Brenne.
Vernou is a flourishing village of close upon
two thousand inhabitants, and its history dates
as far back as the days of Saint Perpet, who
is said to have built the parish church about
the year 480.   The northern wall of the
principal nave of the present building being

built of courses of small stones can well be given that date; but other parts are more recent. The semicircular doorway, with its quaintly ornamented archivolts, resting on columns with sculptured capitals, belongs to the eleventh century, whilst other portions are attributable to the twelfth. Another proof of the great antiquity of Vernou is shown by the remains of a Gallo-Roman or Merovingian building which goes by the name of the Palace of Pepin the Short. Before leaving for Jallanges we also saw, on an open space to the right of the church, an ancient elm, several yards in circumference, and so decrepit that the village blacksmith has had to furnish it with iron girdles to prevent it from utterly collapsing. We found, on inquiry, that it was known as Sully's elm, because of the tradition that it was one of those trees which he planted in various parts of France in 1598 on the occasion of the publication of the Edict of Nantes. From within the decayed bole of this aged elm, a younger tree has shot up stout and strong, as though, with its fresh young branches, to protect its great-great-grandfather from the inclemencies of the weather, and at the same time to keep ever green the recollection of the edict which marked

the political reconciliation of Catholic and
Protestant.

The Château of Jallanges lies at a distance of some three miles from Vernou in
the midst of delightful grounds and a wood.
Historically, the story of this sixteenth
century manor-house in brick and stone is
a very meagre one, since the records contain
little else than a list of its owners. As a
pleasant country residence, therefore, you must
be content to regard it, getting what satisfaction is possible rather from its present than its
past. The domain of Jallanges was in the
possession of René du Perray, a knight-
banneret, as far back as the thirteenth century ;
but the first owner of the present château was
Nicolas Gaudin, Treasurer to the Queen and
Mayor of Tours, who possessed it from
1503 to 1510. In 1515 it was in the hands
of Guillaume Barthélemy, Comptroller of
Finances for Brittany, and from him it passed,
during the next hundred years or so, to various
owners, whose names need not be specially
mentioned. The next owner of importance
was Denis le Royer, a counsellor of the
Parliament of Paris, who held it, however,
only three years, from 1640 to 1643, when
it became the property of Jean de Mons, the

THE CHÂTÉAU OF JALLANGES

THE BILLIARD-ROOM AT JALLANGES

CHÂTEAU OF JALLANGES: A SCULPTURED DOORWAY

King's Secretary.   Then, in 1648, came René
Peyrat, the King's Steward, in whose family
it remained for twenty-six years.   Nicolas
Lefebvre, a counsellor of the Parliament of
Brittany, came into possession, in fact, in 1672 ;
and for more than one hundred years the
château remained in the hands of members
of his family, the last one to possess it being
Pierre Claude Lefebvre de la Falluère, who,
on the 9th of Floreal, in the Year VI, had the
sorrow of seeing it sold by the nation.   The
owners of more modern times include members
of the Salleyx, Bizemont, Contades, and
Meignan families.   The château was restored
by Count Jules de Contades, and the present
owner is M. J. Meignan.

The most decorative façade of the château
is that facing the courtyard.   Built, as I have
said above, of brick and stone, a highly
pleasing combination, its ornamental effect is
increased still more by a diapered pattern of
diamonds formed by the use of bricks of
different shades of red.   Simple though these
means are, they suffice, with hardly any other
adjunct, to produce an admirable result, and
one experiences no sense of loss from the fact
that sculpture has been sparingly used.   Leaving out of account its crocketed gables and

dormer-windows, and the carved grotesques
on each side of the upper portion of the other
windows, its only really noteworthy piece of
work is the sculptured doorway of the tower
which, situated in the middle of the façade,
contains the staircase leading to the various
storeys of the building. The front of the
other side of the house is decidedly less
ornamental, but it has an advantage over the
former in its outlook: a view of a tennis-court
and park-land, framed between magnificent
cedars.

Apart from the contents of the Château of
Jallanges, its interior, which I suspect has
undergone many changes since the sixteenth
century, calls for little mention. Indeed, but
two things particularly attracted our attention:
the painted ceiling in the billiard - room,
and an exquisitely carved mantelpiece of
hard, fine-grained stone in one of the bedrooms. But on the subject of the furniture,
tapestries, and other works of art with which
M. Meignan has embellished his country
home, many pages might be written if it
entered into the scope of this book to describe
them.

The pleasing memories of that excursion
to Vernou and Jallanges formed a fitting con-

clusion to our sojourn at Tours, which we left, only a few days later,—though not without a tinge of regret as we bade farewell to our cottage,—in order to continue our journey down the Loire.

CHAPTER V

DOWN THE LOIRE: AT LUYNES, CINQ-MARS, AND LANGEAIS

A FEW miles from Tours, in a hollow sheltered by the wooded, vine-clad hillside which skirts the right bank of the river as far as St. Patrice, lies the village of Luynes. Neither more nor less picturesque than many another Loire-side village which possesses old houses and rock-dwellings, I do not think we should have lingered there whilst on our way to Langeais, where we had an appointment to visit one of the most important of the châteaux of Touraine, but for the fact that a grim-looking castle of the very type associated with feudal times towered on a hill above steep, narrow streets and an ancient wooden market. It was a clear sunny morning, after a night of rain, with cumulus clouds scudding in a fresh breeze across a deep blue sky; and as the rays of the sun enveloped the castle's pepper-caster towers

and its ivy-covered base the picture was
indeed alluring. So we descended into the
village and, near a quaint market-place,
mounted towards the castle by means of
several flights of steps cut in the hillside.
This unusual approach—it is even more novel
than that at Amboise — traverses former
defensive works, and leads, almost in a
straight line, to the entrance of the château.
There, a bridge crosses the remains of a
moat, overgrown with shrubs and grass and
weeds ; and a few steps farther, through an
ever wide-open portal, brings one into the
courtyard, or, more strictly speaking, castle
garden. Viewed from this point, the
Château of Luynes presents a less aggressive
appearance than it does from below, and it
then becomes obvious that it was built at
two different periods. The fortress-like
towers frowning on the valley of the Loire
date, in fact, from the fifteenth century,
whereas the portion in brick and stone
belongs to the more ornamental and elegant
period of the Renaissance.

Luynes did not always bear the name it
does to-day ; at the end of the eleventh
century it was called Maillé. Moreover, at
that time, also, a castle stood on the hill and

commanded the valley. But, strong though it was, it was finally taken and destroyed by one of the counts of Anjou, who, according to the charter which mentions the exploit, devastated the whole country. However, the position was too good strategically to remain unoccupied for very long, and about 1106 Hardouin of Maillé, who was the first to bear that title, built a second fortress, which, in its turn, was supplanted by the present castle. The change in name dates from 1619, when Charles Albert of Luynes, Keeper of the Seals under Louis XIII, purchased the château and began its enlargement and restoration. Since then it has never left the possession of his descendants. But they can, I imagine, have got little satisfaction out of it, apart from the feeling of pride which a family property engenders. It is ill-suited for a residence, and, though we were told in the village that the present Duke of Luynes is having its rooms restored and put into a fit state for habitation, it is hardly likely that he will pass more than a few weeks there each year during the shooting season. The interior, we found, was closed to visitors, so, without any regrets, we turned our attention to what is to be

seen in the courtyard and, above all, to the
fine view of the valley and the river which
can be obtained from a little terrace to the
left, near an ancient well, and from the
summit of the massive northern and eastern
walls of the castle.

Little more than half-way between Luynes
and Langeais stand two other ancient buildings
which likewise must not be overlooked by
those who travel along the banks of the
Loire. The more interesting is the Pile of
Cinq-Mars, a solid square tower thirty yards
in height, and varying in breadth from five
and a half yards at its base to four and a
half yards at its summit. At what date and
for what purpose this curious construction
was erected is a problem which has been dis-
cussed by archæologists for nearly a century,
but without finding a solution, though the
general belief is that the Pile is of Roman
origin, and that it commemorates some long
since forgotten event in Roman history.
The other building is the castle of the same
name, or rather its remains,—two cylindrical
towers and portions of a huge wall. It was
formerly the ancestral home of Henri Coëffier
de Ruzé, that young favourite of Louis XIII
who had the temerity to conspire against

Richelieu, and who, as a result, was beheaded at Lyons on September 12, 1642. Alfred de Vigny made him the hero of a novel, which should have an interest for you, if only for the reason that it was inspired by Scott's historical romances. The Castle of Cinq-Mars, which was dismantled by Richelieu, must at one time have been a formidable stronghold, judging by its stout towers and splendid military position, which is very similar to that of Luynes. It is now put to the most peaceful of uses. A little colony of houses has clustered around its base ; its sides have been utilised by the vine-growers and small farmers of the village as a convenient support for sheds and store-houses ; and the interior of its grounds has been transformed into fruit gardens.

Once more on the road, through a district of vineyards and orchards and rich pasture-land, diversified, now and then, by a landscape in which tall poplars were the dominating feature, we soon came within sight of the dark slate roofs of the Château of Langeais. A cluster of gray houses with narrow winding streets nestles at the base of a number of small hills, intersected with wooded gorges, through one of the deepest and most

LANGEAIS FROM THE BANKS OF THE LOIRE

picturesque of which babbles the little river
Roumer. In the midst of the village and
on a hillock which entirely dominates it,
rise the massive towers of the château, with
its conical slate roofs and machicolated
cornice. The huge structure is gray and
severe, as becomes a building constructed for
defence, and it commands an admirable
position overlooking the plain, through
which the Loire — a former natural protection against the enemy—flows on its
stately course. Fresh from visiting Blois,
or any other castle of Touraine distinguished
by the richness of its ornamentation, you
may be disappointed on first seeing the
Château of Langeais. But the impression
will not be a lasting one, thoughtful consideration of this masterpiece of military
architecture of the fifteenth century soon
convincing you that it has a special beauty
of its own. In its simplicity and severity
there is an air of majesty which no other
château of this part of France possesses.

Crossing the drawbridge at the main
entrance in the Rue Gambetta, we found
ourselves in the courtyard of the castle and
face to face with the imposing ruins of a
donjon, the history of which is closely

connected with that of Langeais and its
château. It was built in 984 by Count Fulk
of Anjou, surnamed the Black Falcon, whose
portrait has been so admirably drawn by J. R.
Green in his *History of the English People*.
"Fulk Nerra, Fulk the Black," he writes, "is
the greatest of the Angevins, the first in whom
we can trace the marked type of character
which their house was to preserve with a fatal
constancy through two hundred years. He
was without natural affection. In his youth
he burned a wife at the stake, and legend told
how he led her to her doom decked out in
her gayest attire. In his old age he waged
his bitterest war against his son, and exacted
from him when vanquished a humiliation
which men reserved for the deadliest of their
foes. 'You are conquered, you are conquered!'
shouted the old man in fierce exultation, as
Geoffrey, bridled and saddled like a beast of
burden, crawled for pardon to his father's feet.
In Fulk first appeared the low type of super-
stition which startled even superstitious ages
in the early Plantagenets. Robber as he was
of church lands, and contemptuous of ecclesiastical censures, the fear of the judgment drove
Fulk to the Holy Sepulchre. Barefoot, and
with the stroke of the scourge falling heavily

on his shoulders, the Count had himself
dragged by a halter through the streets of
Jerusalem, and courted the doom of martyr-
dom by his wild outbursts of penitence. He
rewarded the fidelity of Hubert of Le Mans,
whose aid saved him from utter ruin, by
entrapping him into captivity and robbing
him of his lands. He secured the terrified
friendship of the French King by dispatching
twelve assassins to cut down before his eyes
the minister who had troubled it. Familiar
as the age was with treason and rapine and
blood, it recoiled from the cool cynicism of
his crimes, and believed the wrath of Heaven
to have been revealed against the union of the
worst forms of evil in Fulk the Black. But
neither the wrath of Heaven nor the curses of
men broke with a single mishap the fifty years
of his success. . . . Cool-headed, clear-sighted,
quick to resolve, quicker to strike, Fulk's
career was one long series of victories over his
rivals. He was a consummate general, and
he had the gift of personal bravery which was
denied to some of his greatest descendants.
To these qualities of the warrior he added a
power of political organisation, a capacity for
far-reaching combinations, a faculty of states-
manship, which became the heritage of the

Angevins, and lifted them as high above the intellectual level of the rulers of their time as their shameless wickedness degraded them below the level of man." Constructed of courses of stone in the Gallo-Roman style, so much admired by archæologists, Fulk's fortress was one of several advanced strongholds which he built when planning the conquest of Touraine, and additional traces of his defences can still, here and there, be found in the park which stretches at its feet.

The park also contains the perfectly preserved foundations of a twelfth century basilica, which, under the name of the Chapel of Our Saviour, was built by that Count of Anjou and Touraine—Fulk v, surnamed the Younger— who took part in the First Crusade and married Millicent, daughter of Baldwin ii, King of Jerusalem, whom he was to succeed. On his return to Langeais he brought back certain relics from the Holy Sepulchre and the Saviour's manger, and it was to hold these that he built this basilica within the enceinte of the fortress. Its foundation was the object of a donative charter which he signed in 1118.

But, apart from this important event in the religious annals of Langeais, there is another and equally good reason for mentioning Fulk v.

His son married Matilda, daughter of
Henry I, King of England, and their children
were Geoffrey and Henry Plantagenet, the
latter of whom became King of England, and
who was the father of Richard the Lion-
Hearted, who in his turn was King of England,
Count of Touraine, and Lord of Langeais.

After the murder of Arthur of Brittany, in
1203, and the consequent confiscation of John
Lackland's possessions, the Langeais fortress
became Crown property, though it was many
times granted to private individuals as a reward
for services to the King. Among these, during
the thirteenth century, the most picturesque
figure is undoubtedly that of Pierre de la
Brosse, who raised himself from the position
of barber-surgeon to that of Prime Minister.
Louis IX presented him with Fulk's fortress,
and he made great improvements to it. His
humble birth and the extraordinary favour in
which he was held by the King greatly excited
the jealousy of the nobility, who sought his
ruin. Continuing their feud during the reign
of Philip the Bold, the King's second wife,
Mary of Brabant, and her friends accused him
of holding treasonable intercourse with the
King of Castille, who was then at war with
France. Philip paid little heed to the accusa-

tion, but Pierre de la Brosse did, and waited
for an opportunity to lodge a counter-com-
plaint. The King's son, by his former wife,
dying shortly afterwards, Pierre de la Brosse
dropped a hint that the Queen might have
poisoned her stepson. This was quite in
accordance with the spirit of the times, and
so also was the means which the King took
to discover the Queen's guilt or innocence.
In a nunnery, in a distant part of France,
lived a nun who was supposed to possess the
gift of prophecy, and two envoys—one of
whom was a relative, and the other a friend
of de la Brosse—were sent to lay the matter
before her, and ask her opinion. It is said
that they tried to bribe her to proclaim the
Queen guilty ; but she was too shrewd to
imperil her professional reputation as a sooth-
sayer, so replied in one of those ambiguous
phrases which have been favoured by all
oracles since the days of Delphi. The King
read it as a proof of the Queen's innocence,
and remembering the former charge against
Pierre de la Brosse, condemned him to death.
He was hanged at Montfaucon, outside Paris,
on June 30, 1278.

From that time until 1466 there were only
governors, or castellans, at Langeais. Mean-

while, however, the steady invasion of Touraine
by the English brought about the capture of
the castle in 1427, and it was not until the
days of Joan of Arc that the province was
definitely freed from the foreign yoke.

As soon as Charles VII had rid himself of
the English, he turned his attention to the
interior organisation of his kingdom, and it
is a noteworthy fact that Langeais, in April
1453, when he issued a decree calling upon
the law officers of the Crown to draw up the
"Customs, Ways, and Usages of Touraine,"
was chosen by him as their meeting-place.
This great work was not completed until
1461.

It was about this time, in the early years of
the reign of Louis XI, that the building of
the present château was commenced, on the
King's behalf, by Jean Bourré, his Comptroller
of Finances for Normandy. If a bad man,
and in some senses not a good King, Louis
thoroughly understood the art of kingcraft.
In the wars with the barons in his early days,
he had learned by experience the value of a
powerful castle at a critical juncture, for it
was to the Castle of Montlhéry, near Paris,
that he owed his throne if not his life. Like
Fulk the Black, he was a good strategist, and

saw the value of the position of Langeais, and
that a strong castle there, held by a retainer
in whom he could trust implicitly, would,
in a great measure, protect him from all
attacks coming from the west, when he was in
Touraine.   His choice of the man who super-
intended the construction of the château was,
too, a good one ; for Jean Bourré, who was
an earnest lover of art, especially when it was
displayed in the form of fine houses, had had
much experience in the building of châteaux.
It is recorded by one who was almost his
contemporary that he " erected and constructed
many fine castles and pleasure houses, such as
Langès, Longué, Jarzé, Vaulz, Couldray, and
Antrammes, near Laval."   Some, such as
Langeais, were for the King ; others, as
the Château of Plessis-du-Vent, which was
begun the year after Langeais and approached
completion in 1472, were for himself.   In
building the Château of Langeais he saw that
the work was carried out not only with
rapidity, which explains the remarkable unity
in the style of its architecture, but also with
great thoroughness.   The materials used—
notably the chestnut woodwork—were excellent in quality, and have so well resisted
the effects of time that the château is to-day

LANGEAIS: FAÇADE FACING THE COURTYARD

LANGEAIS: ANNE OF BRITTANY'S ROOM

certainly one of the finest examples of the
military architecture of the Middle Ages in
existence.

In placing the château opposite the castle
of Fulk the Black, says the Abbé Bossebœuf,
who is our principal authority on the subject
of Langeais and its ancient buildings, it was
the architect's intention to connect them by
two fortified lines crowning the hill's double
escarpment. He first of all built the fortress,
properly so called, consisting of a *corps de logis*,
stretching from north to south, and flanked by
two towers on the side facing the street, with
a drawbridge protected by an outer wall. To
the north the ramparts rose perpendicularly
above the moat, and in a southerly direction
the building was terminated, as was usually
the case, by a wall four yards in thickness.
The château proper was then constructed,
towards the south, a third round tower, similar
in dimensions to the others, being placed at
the far corner. The building was continued
at right angles in a westerly direction. The
château was defended by a magnificent way of
the rounds, one hundred and forty-two yards
six inches long, and from thirty-nine and a
half inches to fifty-one and a half inches
in breadth, with two hundred and seventy

machicolations. The façade facing the courtyard did not require to be so strongly fortified,
and therefore was unprovided with either
round towers or a *chemin de ronde*. Notwithstanding the somewhat irregular manner in
which the two parts of the château were
joined, this façade, with its three hexagonal
towers which serve as staircases, its finely
sculptured doorways, ornamented with superb
wrought-iron knockers, and its mullioned
windows with carved stems and other decorative details, presents a most harmonious appearance. The middle portion of the château
is composed of four storeys containing numerous
bedrooms ; the right wing, on the other hand,
has only three, and contains the large halls.
There are three series of windows, arranged
symmetrically one above the other, the narrow
ones having transoms and the others, which
are nearly two yards in breadth, both transoms
and mullions. The right wing, which lies
east and west, has a somewhat unfinished
appearance, owing to the fact, which was
brought to light by recent excavations, that
it was formerly terminated by a chapel
destroyed during the Revolution.

With the names of the principal owners of
the Chateau of Langeais history has dealt

kindly. But there is one name which it has failed to hand down—that of its architect. The accounts, containing details of expenditure and the names of workmen engaged in its construction, have been lost. Of its very early history, therefore, little more is known than that it was commenced about 1465, in which year Bourré was granted letters patent of nobility and the Captaincy of Langeais, and that the accounts were kept by Jean Briçonnet, the King's treasurer, who lived in a small house in the Rue de la Longue-Echelle. Unknown though its architect is, however, it is certain his work had an important influence on the architecture of the early part of the reign of Louis XI. The Château of Plessis-du-Vent bears a rather striking resemblance to that of Langeais, and there can be no doubt that both castles were planned by the same architect. Jean Bourré was evidently satisfied with the way he had done his work at Langeais, so employed him to draw up the plans of his own château. Coudray-Montpensier and Rigny-Ussé, not to mention other châteaux in various parts of France, also bear traces of the movement which was inaugurated by the man employed by Louis' favourite.

9

Jean Bourré resigned the Captaincy of Langeais several years before his death, which occurred shortly after 1505, and the château then came into the possession of princes of the royal blood. Its interior decoration was completed by the son of the celebrated Bastard of Orleans, Francis of Orleans, Count of Danois and Longueville, who, by letters given at Montargis on July 2, 1466, obtained the domain from Louis XI, and who is credited with the construction of two of the castle's finest mantelpieces. These, which are in the large halls on the ground-floor and first-floor, are beautifully ornamented, in one case with extremely naive heads quaintly placed in the crenelles of a miniature battlement, and a sculptured design of vine and holly ; in the other with blind Gothic arcades and a trefoil decoration.

From the family of the princes of Orleans the château passed into that of the princes of Bourbon. On the marriage of Louis of Bourbon to Joan of France, Louis XI's natural daughter by Marguerite de Sassenage, he received " the fortress and château of Langeais," in March 1473, as a dowry. But he does not appear to have left on the castle any mark of his presence. On the other hand, the

finest parts of the parish church are due to
him : the steeple, which is one of the most
remarkable in Touraine, and the Gothic
sacristy with its vaulted roof and prismatic
mouldings on the central pendentive of which
is his escutcheon—three fleurs-de-lis, or, field
azure, baton gules.

The time was now drawing near when the
Château of Langeais was to be the scene of
the event which, amongst all others in its
varied history, has made it famous : the
marriage of Charles VIII and Anne of Brittany,
in 1491. When a child, Charles had been
engaged to Margaret of Austria, the daughter
of Maximilian, Emperor of Germany ; whilst
Maximilian had been betrothed by proxy to
Anne. But Anne of Beaujeu, the daughter
of Louis XI, who acted as Regent during
Charles' minority, forthwith began to use
the great political skill which she had in-
herited from her astute father. According to
Brantôme, " Charles having perceived that it
was not well to have so powerful a lord
within his kingdom, deprived Maximilian of
the said Anne and married her." In spite
of the opposition which the Duchess of
Brittany at first showed to the marriage, the
affair was carried out with such cleverness,

and troops were advanced on her possessions
with such timeliness, that she consented to
become Queen of France.

Accompanied by Arthur of Montauban,
Bishop of Bordeaux, and Chancellor of
Brittany, the Sire de Coëtquen, and John III
of Pontbriant, Anne arrived at Langeais "in
a travelling dress of cloth and velvet, trimmed
with a hundred and thirty-nine sable skins,"
and on a palfrey adorned with three ells of
crimson velvet. She was pretty—or at least
had the beauty of youth, and Brantôme describes her black eyes and well-marked eye-
brows, long black hair, fresh complexion, and
dimpled chin ; and the only defect he noticed
was that one leg was a trifle shorter than the
other, which he is careful to add is hardly a
defect at all, for it was also the case with
many "beauteous and virtuous dames" with
whom he was acquainted. Her wedding
gown displayed a rare magnificence ; it was
made of cloth of gold, embroidered with gold,
and trimmed with one hundred and sixty
sable skins, and cost a sum of money which,
even in these days of expensive dress, would
be regarded with astonishment.

The marriage contract, which was drawn
up by Pierre Bonneau, the Apostolic notary,

and Guy Leclerc, the crown notary, was
signed in the room of the château now
known as the Salle de Anne de Bretagne.
Its principal clauses stipulated the reunion of
Brittany to France, and, in order to make
this doubly sure, the obligation on the part
of the Queen, should the King die without
issue, to marry his successor,—a strange
condition which was actually carried out.
The nuptial benediction was pronounced by
the Bishop of Angers, it is believed in the
chapel which once terminated the south-west
wing of the château ; and in the presence of
the Duke of Orleans,—the future Louis XII
and her second husband, — the Prince of
Orange, the Duke of Bourbon, the Count of
Angoulême, the Count of Foy, the Count
of Vendôme, and William of Rochefort,
Chancellor of France. The bridegroom, then
in his twentieth year, was, the chronicler tells
us, "short, sickly looking, and extremely
thin," but nevertheless had a "handsome,
gentle, and agreeable face." As to the date
of the ceremony, it was performed in
December, but historians are not quite agreed
as to the exact day, which was probably the
thirteenth of the month. Whether this was
an unlucky day, or whether, as Brantôme

thinks, the betrothal with Maximilian was
really binding, and ought not to have been
ignored in the off-hand fashion it was, the
union of Charles and Anne was not fortunate.
All her children died young, and she was left
a widow in less than seven years. Dunois,
who was one of the principal parties in
arranging the match, fell dead from his horse
in a fit of apoplexy, a few months after the
wedding. On the other hand, there was an
important set-off against these personal
troubles in the fact that Brittany became
henceforth a part of France, and an end was
put to the wars which had long devastated
both countries.

A rapid review of the next three centuries
will now adequately cover the history of
Langeais. First of all, I think you must
consider as a legend the assertion that the
château, at the beginning of the sixteenth
century, belonged to Cardinal du Bellay, the
friend and protector of Rabelais. The Du
Bellay family owned the Château of Langey,
in the department of Eure-et-Loir, and not
that of Langeais. Moreover, the charming
" Maison de Rabelais," which is opposite the
castle, cannot, strictly speaking, have been
inhabited by the immortal writer, though it

is quite possible he may have visited it. By
letters patent dated September 16, 1547,
Henry II gave the lordship of Langeais, in
return for services, to the Duke of Somma,
one of the favourites of Francis I. Charles
IX received hospitality there on November 19, 1565. Louis XIII, descending the
Loire to Saumur, landed at the port of
Langeais in October 1627, dined at the
château, and, according to the report of an
eye-witness, Dr. Herouard, who never left
him, "undressed at nine o'clock, got into
bed at half-past nine, prayed, and then slept
until six in the morning." About this time
the castle, which up to then had been in the
possession of but temporary owners, definitely
ceased to belong to the Crown, and Louise
of Lorraine, the daughter of the celebrated
Duke of Guise, became its absolute owner in
1631. But she sold it soon afterwards for
59,300 livres to Antoine Coëffier de Ruzé,
Marquis of Effiat, Baron of Cinq-Mars and
Superintendent of Finances, whose son Henry
I have already mentioned. One of the lords
of Langeais whose name throws the most
glory on the château during the second half
of the seventeenth century is the Duke of
Mazarin, in whom the Cardinal found so

many good qualities that he gave him his name and his niece, Hortense Mancini, with a dowry of twenty-eight million livres. In 1765, the Effiat family sold the castle and its grounds to Baron de Champchevrier for 27,000 livres ; but in the following year Marie Charles Albert, Duke of Luynes, obtained letters patent authorising him to exercise the right of feudal repurchase. His son, Duke Louis Joseph, remained owner of the castle during the entire revolutionary period, and to him is due its preservation, the only concessions he consented to make being the removal of the coats of arms which ornamented some of the chimney-pieces, and the destruction of the chapel. He sold the château in 1798 to M. Charles Moisant, of Tours, for 170,000 francs. The new owner, however, took no care whatever of it ; indeed, he left it in such a state of abandonment that some of the villagers used it as a place for storing their wood and drying their clothes, whilst others, with a view to economy in building, constructed their houses against the château. As to the park, they divided it into sixty plots, which they planted with vines. And the municipality itself could find nothing better to do than to transform the

THE GUARDROOM AT LANGEAIS

THE SALON DES FLEURS AT LANGEAIS

large room on the ground-floor into a stable
for the gendarmes !

Such was the lamentable state of this fine
old castle in 1833 when M. Christophe Baron,
a Paris lawyer, was struck, whilst on his way
to Nantes, by its beauty and its admirable
position. He decided to purchase it. But
it was not until April 22, 1839, that he
was able to accomplish his desire. From that
year dates the château's new lease of life.
Practical man of the world that he was, and
endowed, withal, with a keen sense of humour,
he inaugurated his ownership by two most
original measures. He informed the owners
of the houses abutting on the château that he
was disposed to purchase them for triple
their value if evacuated the first year, for
double their value the year following, and
for their exact value the third year. But if,
at the end of three years, they had not accepted his proposal, he intended to set the law
in motion and turn them out without paying
a penny. The result was that he obtained
almost all the houses at their market value,
for the majority of their owners — peasant
like—stubbornly insisted on remaining where
they were until the very last moment. As
to the holders of the vineyards in the park,

he called a meeting of them one Sunday
afternoon. A notary read a deed of sale
offering them twice the value, but containing
a final clause stipulating that the sixty owners
should be unanimous in accepting the offer.
Left to themselves, the peasant-proprietors
began to discuss the matter. Calm at first,
the meeting soon became noisy ; then the
sound of blows was heard, followed by cries ;
and, finally, it was in a perfect uproar. However, towards evening they had come to a
mutual understanding and the sixty signatures
were affixed on the agreement. Meanwhile,
M. Baron, whose hobby was archæology,
began to restore the château ; and, though
his taste and knowledge may not always
have been applied to the best purpose, lovers
of the old castles of Touraine are under a
debt of gratitude to him for aiding in the
preservation of so fine a piece of architecture.

To others, wealthier and more competent,
was reserved the task—nearly thirty years
after M. Baron's death—of bringing the
Château of Langeais to its present splendid
state. During our many wanderings in
Touraine we never met with a finer example
of skilful restoration, and I doubt if it would be

possible to find a more convincing one anywhere. Mr. Henry James, in his book of
impressions entitled, *A Little Tour in France*,
says that the apartments of the Château of
Langeais, " though they contain many curious
odds and ends of antiquity, are not of first-
rate interest." But that was written over
twenty years ago, in the days of white-washed
walls and deal flooring, and since then the
interior of the castle, as regards furnishing and
mural decoration, has undergone a complete
transformation. Since then the Château of
Langeais has come into the possession of M.
Jacques Siegfried, a wealthy man of commerce,
inspired with a love of ancient art, and he
has so changed it, with the collaboration of
Madame Siegfried, an equally enthusiastic lover
of the past, that the fifteenth century lives
again in its ancient rooms. On purchasing
the property in 1886, he found that, although
the exterior was in a very fair state of preservation, many alterations had to be made
before it could be said to present the aspect it
had in the fifteenth century. Certain errors
in restoration, dating from the time of M.
Baron's ownership, had to be corrected.
Details in the architecture of the roof were
changed, and an anachronism in the form of

a blue clock face was removed. There was not an old plan, ancient document, or book describing the château's appearance in 1465 which M. Lucien Roy did not seek out and study; and whilst this well-known architect was engaged on the architectural side of restoration, a number of eminent artists and collectors were giving their assistance in restoring the thirty halls and rooms of the castle to their ancient splendour. The former white-washed walls were covered by M. Charles Lameire with beautiful decorative paintings, done by the encaustic process, and inspired by fifteenth century tapestries and the designs in the *Book of Hours* of Anne of Brittany, a copy of which is in the château. MM. Bonnaffé, Foulc, Emile Peyre, and Spitzer, well-known collectors, aided M. Siegfried in ransacking the archives of large public libraries in search of useful facts, in copying old documents containing details of interior decoration, and in making purchases at sales even in the most distant parts of the country. No genuine specimen of fifteenth and sixteenth century work was too unimportant to be let slip, if it made a fitting addition to the Langeais collections. One class of antique, however, was debarred by

M. Siegfried: nothing that he purchased had any connection with warfare.

In an exceedingly pleasant room on the ground-floor, called the Salon des Fleurs, our attention was attracted by a very effective piece of mural decoration by M. Lameire, representing mallow flowers and upright branches of cherries; and in the magnificent guardroom we noticed a frieze by the same artist, composed of the arms of Anne of Brittany interwoven with her motto: POTIUS MORI QUAM FŒDARI. These arms, which are repeated around the room, are accompanied by figures of greyhounds with collars and ermined *mouchoirs*. The mural decoration in these two rooms may be taken as an example of the conscientious work of restoration which has been accomplished throughout the château. Appropriateness is the note which you meet on every side. Take the case, for instance, of the beautiful tiled floors, all of which were specially made for the château, and at what an expenditure may be imagined when I say that the tiling of no two rooms is alike.

Another of the glories of Langeais is its furniture. This can be divided into two classes: genuine fifteenth century work and copies from ancient models. As far as possible,

M. and Madame Siegfried have endeavoured
to find authentic pieces ; but when neither love
nor money could obtain them they had first-
rate copies made from examples in museums.
For instance, an extremely beautiful cupboard
with finely wrought metal ornamentations in
the guardroom is a copy from an ancient
locker in the Church of St. Germain
l'Auxerrois, in Paris ; but the two stalls on the
opposite side of the same room are genuine
fifteenth century work. The latter, which
were formerly in the Church of Argues-la-
Bataille, are superbly proportioned, and the
carving of their backs and canopies is a
masterpiece of execution. Other beautifully
carved stalls and seats are also to be seen in
the Salle des Gardes, the Salle de Anne de
Bretagne, and the Salon des Fleurs. In the
last-named room, by the bye, is a curious fire-
screen, painted in grey camaïeu, which was
formerly in the possession of Louise of Vaudemont, the wife of Henry III. It formed part of
the furniture in the mourning-room (*chambre de
deuil*) occupied by the widowed Queen at the
Château of Chenonceaux, of which she was
the owner.

The Château of Langeais also contains a
good selection of cabinets and chests. In one

of its many charming bedrooms is a particularly fine example of a fifteenth century *bahut*, and in the same room are several other authentic specimens of works of that period, notably a Spanish torch-holder, a fragment of German tapestry, representing a person riding on horseback, and a virgin in gilded wood of French workmanship ; whilst in another bedroom are two Italian chests ornamented with paintings and bearing the arms of the Chigi family.

As regards the beds, the division into genuine antiques and copies still holds good. I noticed, however, that most of them are specimens of thirteenth century work,—a deviation from the rule to furnish the château in the style of the fifteenth and sixteenth centuries which has its advantages from an æsthetic point of view, the beds of the fifteenth century being cumbersome and not over pretty, whereas those of the thirteenth were small and elegant. "The beds of this period," says Viollet-le-Duc, "were habitually composed of a sort of balustrade placed on four feet, with an opening in the middle of one of the sides to enable the person wishing to sleep to slip between the clothes without effort. These beds were low,—the height of

a sofa. The sleeper's head was raised by
several pillows placed one on the top of
another." Metal had been completely abandoned in favour of wood in their manufacture.
As to decoration, this is clearly shown in many
ancient documents, and the carving and even
colouring of thirteenth century beds can be
reproduced with almost scrupulous accuracy.
One of those at Langeais is, indeed, a copy of
a bed illustrated and described by Viollet-le-
Duc, who in turn copied it from a thirteenth
century manuscript, in the National Library,
containing the *Histoire de Saint Græl* and
other stories translated from the Latin.
Hangings and testers were often of great
richness and beauty, and frequently bore
symbolical emblems, such as those which are
to be seen at Langeais : " Potius mori quam
fœdari," " Spera in Deo," " Post tenebras
spera lucem," " Prye à cant d'oiseau," " A
vaillant (cœur) rien impossible." We noticed,
too, that their curtains were tucked up in
accordance with ancient custom.

Equally as important as the furniture, if not
more so, are the tapestries, which add so much
to the richness of colouring of the château's
interior. The first to attract our attention
were two belonging to a series depicting the

A TYPICAL BEDROOM AT LANGEAIS

A PORTION OF THE WAY OF THE ROUNDS AT LANGEAIS

FIFTEENTH CENTURY STALL AT LANGEAIS

"Story of the Holy Sacrament." These
valuable works were purchased by M. Siegfried
in October 1888 at the sale of tapestries at the
Château of Plessis-Macé, in the department
of Maine-et-Loire, and they originally came
from the ancient Abbey of Ronceray, at
Angers. On this Benedictine church being
despoiled at the time of the Revolution, they
found their way to the neighbouring Church
of the Trinity, which sold them to the
Château of Serrant, whence they passed to that
of Plessis-Macé. The complete series was
composed of eleven pieces, in which the
Sacrament was regarded from a triple point of
view: its figures in the Old Testament, its
institution, and the miracles it had occasioned
in the Church. The first and the last are at
Langeais. Where they were made is unknown, but for whom is clearly shown by the
first of the series, since it bears the initials and
arms of Isabelle de la Jaille, who was Lady
Superior of the Abbey of Ronceray from 1505
to 1518. They were given by Louise Leroux,
then *doyenne* of that religious house. M.
Siegfried also owns the first panel of the "Story
of Saint Saturninus," dated 1527, one of a
series of eight tapestries which have an interesting history. Benoît de la Grandière, in a
10

note to one of the last chapters of his *Histoire
des Maires de Tours*, speaks of them as having
been made for Jean Duval and as existing in
the Church of Saint Saturnin at Tours in 1780.
They were given to that church by Jacques
de Beaune-Semblançay, whose house at Tours
has been mentioned in the preceding chapter.
On the outbreak of the Revolution these
beautiful tapestries disappeared, and were
thought to have been destroyed.   Some forty
years ago, however, three of the most important of the series were found in the possession
of a second-hand furniture dealer, who sold
them to the chapter of the Angers Cathedral.
A little over ten years ago a fourth was
discovered in the hands of another dealer, in
the Rue de Vaugirard, in Paris, and after
figuring in the Tours Exhibition of 1891, was
bought by M. Siegfried.   It represents St.
John preaching before a numerous audience,
some seated and others standing, including St.
Saturninus, who is recognisable by his aureole.
The Gothic tapestry in the same room, representing Christ on the cross, the Virgin Mary,
and St. John, dates from the fifteenth century
and was once in the collection of M. Goupil.
But assuredly the most curious of the tapestries
at the Château of Langeais are the series known

as the " Neuf Preux." " Preux " is an old
French word meaning " Hero," and the nine
heroes were Joshua, David, Hector, Cæsar,
Artus, Godfrey of Bouillon, Judas Maccabeus,
Alexander, and Charlemagne. Only the first
six (and a fragment) of these are represented
in the Langeais series. Each hero is the
subject of a quatrain, the portrait of Julius
Cæsar, for instance, being accompanied by the
following lines :

> " Julius Cesar fort renommé je suis
> Qui le fier Pompée ay vaincu et occis
> Et en mes jours empereur de romme fuz
> Six centz ans devant que fut ne jesus." [1]

In the opinion of Mgr. Barbier de Montault,
who has written an exhaustive treatise on
these tapestries, they were made between 1525
and 1540 in La Marche, which possessed two
tapestry manufactories. Before coming into
M. Siegfried's possession they were the
property of M. Reversé, of Saint Maixent,
who purchased them, together with the
Château Chauray, from a M. de Surimeau.
Nothing more is known of the history of six

---

[1] " I am the much renowned Julius Cæsar
Who conquered and killed proud Pompey,
And I was once Emperor of Rome
Six hundred years before Christ was born."

of the most curious tapestries in the world.
In addition to these principal works are others,
notably an interesting panel entitled " Les
Travaux et les plaisirs des Champs," and
another called the "Tapisserie des Paons,"
representing a balustrade with peacocks on a
background of Gothic thistles.

Though exceptionally well off for tapestries,
the Château of Langeais is rather sparsely
provided with pictures. But those that are
there are of the best. One of the bedrooms
is made glorious by the rich colouring and
Lombardian grace of a fresco by Bernardino
Luini, dated 1422, which came from a chapel
in Locarno ; in the Salle de Anne de Bretagne
are contemporary portraits of Charles VIII
and Anne,—two of the very portraits, attached
by hinges, so as to fold, face to face, and
bearing on the back the royal initial K
(Karolus), which were presented by the King
to one of his wedding-guests ; and in the
same room is a Magdalen, by Henner,—the
only modern painting I noticed,—which is
accounted one of the painter's finest works.

Multitudinous art treasures are thus to be
seen on every side. Not the least interesting
are the examples of wrought-iron work.
Here, again, the owner of the château has

been faithful to the ideal with which he set out when he commenced the work of restoration. The beautiful knockers on the doors in the courtyard have already been mentioned, but I would once more draw attention to them, as well as to the decorative bolts with which these fine old doors are studded. At the corners of the hexagonal towers in the courtyard are two interesting torch-holders, but these, unlike the locks and bolts on the inner doors, are also scrupulously accurate copies of fifteenth century models. In the Salle de Anne de Bretagne are two admirable candelabra, copied from a picture by Albert Durer ; and on each side of a doorway at the end of the guardroom are two most elegant Italian tripod stands for holding braziers. There are several examples of old locks, two particularly beautiful ones detached, but most of them fixed on ancient pieces of furniture. Finally, a word should be said for the massive iron firedogs which support huge logs of wood in the broad fireplaces. Those in the guardroom came from the former Château of Chanteloup, and one of another pair was discovered in the Langeais grounds, where it had lain hidden for centuries.

We had a double satisfaction in looking

at the art treasures stored at Langeais, for to
the pleasure which they evoked was added
the joy of knowing that they cannot be
dispersed. Anxious that the result of twenty
years' patient work should be preserved, the
owner has followed the example of the Duc
d'Aumale in the case of Chantilly, and presented the castle and its collections to the
Institute of France, on the condition, naturally,
that he and his wife retain the usufruct
during their lives. In so doing, they hope
not only to prevent the castle from passing
into the hands of others who might close
it to the public, but also that their collections
will in the future form the nucleus for a
still richer museum of fifteenth and sixteenth
century art. In addition to this generous
donation, M. Siegfried has deposited in the
hands of trustees a sum of money sufficient
to produce an income of £500 to pay for
repairs and other annual expenses which may
be incurred in connection with the arrangement of the contents of the castle as a public
museum. What a sense of gladness must be
felt by the connoisseur who knows that his
precious collections will be enjoyed in per-
petuity,—that thousands upon thousands will,
like himself, be carried back by them to

ancient days! Verily the stamp of feudal times is on everything in this wonderful château, and he who, walking through its rooms with timbered ceilings, or sitting in its quaint stone window-seats, could not transport himself for a time to the days of Louis XI and Charles VIII and Anne of Brittany would indeed be a person of little imagination.

CHAPTER VI

DOWN THE LOIRE: AT ST. PATRICE AND PORT BOULET

" I AM positively dying to see the Metsus,"
said my enthusiastic companion as we
travelled along the dusty road towards St.
Patrice and the Château of Rochecotte.
"You know how fond I am of Metsu,
with his wonderful finish, his simply exquisite rendering of the texture of a silken
gown."

"Well, we ought not to be long in arriving
now," I replied. "Since leaving Langeais
I have counted four kilometre posts, so but
three more separate you and your favourite
pictures. I warrant, too, that your patience
will be rewarded by the sight of at least one
work by that other beloved painter of yours,
Gerard Dow. But of course *all* the best
Dutch artists of the seventeenth century will
be represented in the Rochecotte collection.
Wasn't I told that it contained the pick of

THE CHÂTEAU DE ROCHECOTTE

the masterpieces which belonged to the
princes of Courland ? "

"Really ? How splendid ! In that case
I know I shall not be the only one to go
into raptures. I well recollect your idolatry
of Albert Cuyp and of certain Meuse landscapes of his which we saw together years
ago ; and I have not forgotten how you
quoted Walter Pater to me on the subject
of those 'blond' masterpieces. Unless my
memory betrays me, you said that he had
developed 'the latent gold in Rembrandt,'
and 'brought into his native Dordrecht a
heavy wealth of sunshine.' And what about
your old admiration of Ruysdael's forest
scenes, Adrian van Ostade's cottage interiors,
Hobbema's subtle studies of light, and Franz
Hals' harmonies in gray and silver ? I myself
shall enjoy Ruysdael and Hobbema, after I
have finished with Metsu and Dow. But
look !—surely those are the first houses of
the village ?—Yes ; I thought so. Then we
cannot be far from the château now."

Either we had covered the ground with
unwonted celerity, or, my attention being
diverted by riverside beauties, I had mis-
counted the kilometres. At all events, as
we swept round a bend in the road, there

we were at St. Patrice and directly opposite
the ornamental wrought-iron gates of the
Château of Rochecotte. A long, straight,
and rather neglected avenue led us up the
wooded hillside under the lee of which the
village stands; and on almost reaching
the top we caught sight, between the trees
on our right, of the château, a plain and
yet distinctly elegant seventeenth century
building, placed at a point where the eye
can take in an admirable view of the valley
of the Loire, with Ussé and other châteaux
plainly visible on a clear day. Approaching
a columned and escutcheoned entrance, shaded
by an ancient fir tree, I had a premonition
of disappointment on seeing the closed shutters
of the white sunlit façade. Were we going
to find that the Dutch treasures were inexorably guarded against the public eye?
Certainly it looked very much like it, since
we rang the bell again and again without
receiving an answer. At last, when it became
evident that the mansion was unoccupied, I
set off on a journey of exploration amongst
some adjoining outbuildings, and there, received by the fierce barking of a watchdog,
I found the caretaker. Yes; the family was
away, said this respectful, aged man; but if

we liked he would willingly show us over
the château, though he feared it contained
little to interest us. That last observation
of his made us profoundly pity him, for it
was clear he could not be a lover of Dutch
art. After the opening of many doors and
shutters, he feebly led the way from room
to room. This—a room occupying the entire
ground-floor of the right wing of the château—
was the drawing-room, the portraits on the
walls being those of members of the Castellane
family ; here, to the left of the vestibule,
was the library, filling two exceedingly inviting apartments ; and the room adjoining
was the *salle-à-manger*, with more family
portraits on the walls. On the way to the
first-floor he drew our attention to the
wrought-iron balustrade of the staircase,
remarking, " On ne fait pas des choses si bien
aujourd'hui : la main-d'œuvre est trop chère,"
and pointing out that the portraits on the
landing were those of Madame de Sévigné
and her daughter, the former of whom, in
1669, had married François de Castellane,
Comte de Grignan. He next took us into
a succession of bedrooms opening on to an
old-fashioned corridor, hung with more
portraits of Castellanes, and then, partly

retracing our steps and mounting another staircase, into a little gallery to view the interior of the chapel. For some unexplained reason he showed a particular fondness for this chapel, and he enjoined us to see its exterior, which he pronounced, in the reverential tone of voice of an old retainer, to be "très bel et digne d'une grande famille." Not wishing to hurt his feelings we complied, though I fancied I heard my companion, as we followed him outside, heave a little sigh on drawing away from her favourite painters of *genre*. There was some compensation, however, in finding that our *cicerone* was very well informed about this chapel with profusely decorated façade, which, by the bye, is badly in need of restoration. It had been built, he said, by the Duchesse de Dino, in memory of her uncle, Monseigneur le Prince de Talleyrand, who had frequently come over from the Château of Valençay to spend the summer with her at Rochecotte, and its site was that of the very bedroom he had occupied. Talleyrand having made her his heiress, she had come into possession of his papers, including those curious memoirs which he had heard had aroused so much curiosity

THE LIBRARY AT ROCHECOTTE

ROCHECOTTE : THE CHÂTEAU CHAPEL

and discussion,—memoirs which, unfortunately, she had not seen published, since
she died on September 29, 1862, six
years before the date fixed for their
publication. So it was well she had had
the satisfaction of raising this monument to
his name. When it was evident that he
had finished his story, I ventured to suggest
that we should return to the house to
continue our visit. That was as monsieur
and madame pleased, he replied, but there
only remained the second-floor, and that,
he felt sure, would hardly interest them.

"But we have not seen the pictures!" I
exclaimed, a growing suspicion coming over
me.

"What pictures, Monsieur, s'il vous
plaît?"

"Why, the Dutch pictures, of course;
those of the famous Courland collection."

"Ah, Monsieur, now I understand," sadly
responded the old servant. "Alas, Monsieur,
they were taken away a long time ago. And
as to what has become of them I am not quite
certain; but I believe they were divided
among members of the family."

The caretaker had gone to close the château.
Opposite the chapel and under a shady *pergola*,

overgrown with Virginia creeper, we walked
and mused, my companion declaring that this
was even a greater disappointment than that
we had experienced at the Château of Plessis-
les-Tours. Whilst fully agreeing, I did my
best to persuade her that this was one of the
unavoidable *contretemps* of travel, to be met in
that philosophic spirit which all travellers
acquire sooner or later. The casket, it was
true, had been found empty. But did it not
possess a beauty of its own, apart from what
it had once contained ? Moreover, Rochecotte
had a history ; and were not historical recollections—indestructible and irremovable—
almost as precious as works of art ? Among
its associations, for instance, was as romantic
a story as had ever been penned by novelist.
Since she had never heard it, there could be
no more appropriate place than this for its
recital. And thus it happened that, seated
within the cool shade of the bower, I related
the life of the Chouan, Fortuné Guyon, Count
of Rochecotte.

"Fortuné Guyon or Guillon, as the name
is spelt in some records, came of a family
which had owned the Château of Rochecotte
since the beginning of the eighteenth century.
In 1700 its owner was Marie Dublineau, the

wife of René Guyon, who was the Treasurer of France attached to the financial department of Tours ; in 1763 it was in the possession of Louis François Marie Guyon, and about the time to which I am particularly referring it had passed by inheritance into the hands of our hero's father, who, by virtue of letters patent, signed at Versailles in January 1767, was Marquis of Rochecotte. The Marquis, who was also Baron de Colombiers and Seigneur de Boizai and de Vogue, had been a brilliant officer in the Orleans cavalry regiment, and at the time of his son's birth, in 1769, had retired to his château on an income of close upon £2000.

" At an early age Fortuné, whose education during boyhood was entrusted to his father's chaplain, showed himself an apt scholar, and at the same time an adept in all outdoor exercises, especially those of hunting and riding, which he was allowed to practise to his heart's content in the extensive grounds that still surround this château. He likewise had a predilection for arms, and already when a mere boy had decided—greatly influenced, naturally, by the Marquis — to follow his father's old profession. At the conclusion of his studies in Paris, the Duc de Châtelet, who

had come to take a great interest in his
welfare, suggested that he should join the
King's infantry regiment, of which he was
colonel.   Fortuné Guyon, then only seventeen
years of age, immediately accepted the offer,
and, without losing time by first of all going
home, posted straight to Nancy, where his
regiment was in garrison.   Some two years
elapsed before he again saw his father and
sister,—and then only for a few weeks.   The
signs that France was on the eve of Revolution
were becoming more and more frequent,
making it imperative that every soldier should
be at his post.   So the young officer, bitter at
heart, and feeling, as he embraced his father,
that he might never see him again, dragged
himself away from Rochecotte.   The storm
broke soon after his departure.   The meeting
of the National Assembly, the fall of the
Bastille, the women's march to Versailles, and
the Feast of Pikes followed in rapid succession.   Then, in August and September 1790,
came disaffection in the army, the mutiny of
certain regiments, and the Nancy massacre,
the news of which, to use Carlyle's words,
went 'pealing through all France, awakening,
in town and village, in clubroom, messroom,
to the utmost borders, some mimic reflex or

imaginative repetition of the business, always with the angry questionable assertion : It was right. It was wrong.' But the news of the Nancy catastrophe brought in its train more than that : it killed the Marquis of Rochecotte.

"Shortly before hearing of his father's death, Fortuné's regiment had been disbanded and a large number of his fellow-officers had already fled the country. He himself decided to follow their example, and in March 1791 did so, in company with a young nobleman of Touraine, though not until he had once more returned to the Château of Rochecotte to visit his father's grave and make final arrangements for his sister's safety. Proceeding to Oberkirch, in Germany, in the states of Cardinal Prince Louis de Rohan, of diamond necklace fame, he and other royalists formed a company of cavalry which, under the orders of the Prince de Condé, fought with great bravery during the whole of the war against the new masters of France. It soon, however, became evident to Fortuné Guyon that, if the régime was to be overthrown, it could only be done by continuing hostilities in the very heart of the country itself ; so he determined to return home and

11

throw in his lot with the royalist insurgents
of the Vendée or with the Chouans of
western France. Accordingly, in May 1795,
he set off in disguise, accompanied by Comte
Théodore de Bourmont, the Prince de Condé's
aide-de-camp. On reaching Sammarçoles, near
Loudun, Guyon heard that Charette, the
royalist leader on whom he was relying for
assistance, had made peace with the Republican
party, and that Stofflet, another prominent
leader, was about to sign a similar treaty.
Therefore, whilst Comte de Bourmont went
into Brittany, he himself made for Tours.
Passing along the banks of the Loire, he could
not resist the temptation of visiting the ancestral
home. But as he approached the château he
almost failed to recognise it, so many changes
had it undergone during his four years' absence.
Seeing a peasant standing near, he asked him
what had happened. 'The old Marquis of
Rochecotte is dead, Monsieur,' replied the
countryman, 'and his son is an *émigré*. Everything has been sold, and the new owner has
pulled down half of the château to pay for the
remainder. But I can tell you, Monsieur,
he's not at all easy-minded in his new house,
for he has a mortal dread of royalists. In fact,
he's no confidence in the treaty they've just

signed. And there, in my opinion, he's not
far wrong, for it's said they'll soon take up
arms again. But I dare say you yourself
know all about that, since you've doubtless
fought against them and know their qualities ? '
Encouraged by the prospect of renewing
hostilities against those who had robbed
him of his property, Fortuné Guyon hastened
to Poitiers, where one of his uncles, an
ardent royalist named M. d'Ormans, lived ;
and from that time dates the extraordinary
activity which he showed throughout his life
as an insurgent leader in the ancient provinces
of Maine and Touraine.

"Inspired by the insurrectional methods
adopted by the Royalist Agency in Paris,
numerous secret societies, the members of
which called themselves such names as
'Fidèles' and 'Philanthropes,' sprang into
existence through his initiative in the districts
of Mans, Tours, and Poitiers. He put himself
into touch with the rebel organisation which
had been formed at Sillé-le-Guillaume by
L'Hermite and Geslin, two well-known
Chouans. He accompanied his friend De
Bourmont and another royalist named
Vaugiraud to the Belleville camp to attempt
to bring about a reconciliation between Stofflet

and Charette, who now regarded each other
as rivals ; and he took part in a fruitless
attempt to secure for Stofflet part of the ammu-
nition which had been furnished by England
to the other Vendée chief.   And, finally,
in order to create a diversion from the insur-
rection in the Vendée, he dashed hither
and thither in the Sarthe and in the Loir-et-
Cher, inciting the inhabitants of the Cantons
of Château-du-Loir, Villedieu, and Montoire
to revolt.   It was on the occasion of one of
the numerous engagements which he and his
men had at this time with the soldiers of old
General Chalbos, who was in command of
the Republican forces at Tours, that there
occurred one of the many romances of which
his life was composed.   Wounded near Vallon,
his followers carried him to the Château de
Rouillon, not far from Mans, where they
knew he would receive every care at the
hands of its occupants, Madame de Rouillon
and her friend the Vicomtesse de D——.
The latter, indeed, was one of the most
devoted of nurses to Fortuné Guyon, who
showed his gratitude by 'covering with
kisses the pretty hands which tended him.'
Nor did her devotion to him cease after his
recovery and departure.   At the end of July

1796, when Guyon was in Paris on revolutionary business, the charming Viscountess and her friend, seized with a desire to play at being rebels, set off for Mans, and, little suspecting that they were watched by the police, occupied the hiding-places which he had contrived in his flat in that town. News of the escapade came to Fortuné's ears through one of his trusty agents, and he promptly ordered his two friends to return to their château. Whilst deprecating the running of unnecessary risks, he was, however, by no means averse from the most dangerous enterprises, provided that the cause he had at heart stood a chance of being benefited ; and but a year after the occurrence I have just mentioned he had an opportunity of putting the Vicomtesse de D——'s nerve and affection to a severe test. He sent her on a secret mission to England to see Monsieur and get him to forbid J. de Puisaye, another of the royalist leaders, to trespass on his command in Maine. On her return, accompanied by Mademoiselle Guyon, who passed as her *femme de chambre*, the two ladies were arrested at Boulogne. But the intrepid Viscountess was quite equal to the emergency : she managed to escape from

prison disguised in masculine dress, leaving
her 'maid,' who was shortly afterwards
liberated, to follow her.

"The Count of Rochecotte's quarrel with
De Puisaye led to him making a special
journey, shortly after the 18th of Fructidor
Year V, to Blankenburg, where he obtained
from Louis XVIII more extensive authority
over the royalist forces than he had hitherto
had,—probably his rival's post as commander-
in-chief of the insurgents of the west of
France. But, in order to replace De Puisaye
at all effectually, something more was needed,
—the pecuniary assistance of England ; and
to secure that it was necessary to do some
signal service to that country. So he set
to work to organise the escape from prison
of Commodore Sidney Smith, who, on
April 19, 1796, had been captured at Havre,
in company with a Breton nobleman, Jacques
Jean Marie François de Tromelin, and imprisoned in the Temple. The undertaking
was one which necessitated the greatest
coolness and daring, but, aided by a number
of other royalists — Hyde de Neuville,
Phélippeaux, Carlos Sourdat, a dancer named
Boisgirard, Madame de Tromelin, and others,
all of whom daily risked their lives—it met

with entire success.   Whilst Guyon and
some of his friends, armed and disguised,
laid in wait near the entrance to the prison,
ready, if necessary, to use force, others,
dressed as Republican soldiers and provided
with a forged document ordering Sir Sidney
Smith's removal to the Fontainebleau prison,
presented themselves to the Temple authorities
and, without much difficulty, had the prisoner
handed over to them.   Once outside, Sir Sidney
Smith was hurried off to a safe hiding-place
and thence on the road to Havre and home.
Not until a fortnight later, and almost at
the very time that the Commodore was
being enthusiastically received in London,
did the French discover that he had
escaped !

" After so brilliant a service as this, Fortuné
Guyon might well have expected to receive
substantial recognition from the Court of
St. James', and he would, in all probability,
have attained his object through Sir Sidney
Smith's influence had the fates but ordained it.
But he did not even receive the gift of five
hundred pounds which the grateful Commodore
(who forgot not a single one of his rescuers)
sent him.   On June 29, 1798, he was be-
trayed to the police by a Vendée officer,

Richard Duplessis, whom he had formerly made a Knight of St. Louis.

"Seated within the shadow of this château, which its one time owner was never to see again, except in memory, I can call up every detail of the tragic struggle which took place when he was arrested on the Pont Royal in Paris. The first officer to seize him received a fatal poniard thrust; the second a less dangerous wound; the third was killed on the spot. Running in the direction of the Rue de Bac, followed by a number of citizens, Guyon made a vain attempt to escape. 'I am an *émigré*!—not a thief!' he shouted again and again. But the gathering crowd, as he made another dash for life, would not let him go; they brought him to the ground with any missiles they could lay their hands on, and thus, bleeding and half-unconscious, gave him up to the police.

"Though the Count of Rochecotte persisted, in his declarations, in saying that his name was Ulric Néméré, of the department of Puy-de-Dôme, his identity was conclusively proved by Duplessis' evidence, for the traitor pointed out the scar of the wound his benefactor had received near Vollon; and so, shortly afterwards, he was condemned to

death, and—in spite of the Vicomtesse de
D——'s efforts to rescue him—shot on the
Champ-de-Mars. His loss to the royalist
party was irreparable. Many *émigrés* in
London henceforth despaired of the re-
establishment of the monarchy, and Prince
Auguste, on hearing that he was dead,
paid a touching tribute to his many admirable qualities."

"A most interesting story!" exclaimed my
companion, when I had finished. "I am glad
now we came to Rochecotte; your little
romance has quite compensated for the loss
of those pictures. I only wish you could
promise to connect such a one with every
château we visit. I wonder what we shall
find at Réaux? And now, *en route*!"

The Château of Réaux stands at Port-Boulet,
a few miles farther down the Loire. There,
the widening out of the river, whose volume
has been increased by the waters of the Indre,
becomes more and more apparent; it has now
definitely lost that appearance of inoffensive-
ness which is its most marked characteristic
some thirty miles upstream; and the country
in the immediate neighbourhood of its banks
being wilder and more deserted it has the
aspect, in miniature, of one of the broad,

swift-flowing water-courses of the New World. Réaux, which was once called Plessis-Rideau or Plessis-Macé, was built in 1462 by Jean Briçonnet, a King's Councillor, President of the Court of Accounts in Paris, and Mayor of Tours; and it replaced a strongly fortified castle of which little is known save the name. After remaining for nearly two centuries in the Briçonnet family, it was sold, about 1650, by the builder's great-grandson, François de la Beraudière, Marquis de l'Isle-Rouche, to Gédéon Tallemant, who obtained letters patent authorising him to call it the Château of Réaux.

Of all the owners of this delightful manor-house in dark red brick and stone, arranged in a symmetrical pattern,—one of the most decorative, with its framework of greenery and its background of trees, in Touraine,— Tallemant des Réaux, as he was henceforth called, has reflected most glory upon it. He was the eldest son by a second wife of Pierre Tallemant, a man of considerable wealth, and he was born at La Rochelle on November 7, 1619. Like most of the well-to-do young men of the seventeenth century, he travelled in Italy at an early age, and on returning to Paris took his degree

A VIEW OF RÉAUX FROM THE GROUNDS

ENTRANCE TO THE CHÂTEAU DE RÉAUX

THE DRAWING-ROOM

in civil and canonical law, with a view to
entering the magistracy, in accordance with
his father's wishes. But feeling no inclination for such a career, and finding that his
father would allow him very little money,
Gédéon married, in 1646, a wealthy cousin,
Elizabeth de Rambouillet, the daughter of
Nicolas de Rambouillet, his mother's brother.
Relieved from further anxiety over worldly
affairs, he spent the remainder of his life (he
died on November 10, 1692) in the pursuit
of letters, in appearing in fashionable society,
and in looking after the welfare of his family.
He was an assiduous frequenter of the Hôtel
de Rambouillet, that famous rendezvous of
Parisian literature and fashion at 15 Rue
St. Thomas du Louvre, a street now long
since demolished ; and he thus came into close
contact with all the most celebrated people
of the day. "A friend of the Marquise de
Rambouillet," says his biographer, M. Mon-
merqué, "he was surrounded by the most
illustrious members of the nobility and the
most renowned men and women of letters.
He saw this lady—she who was so rightly
celebrated, she who was related to two
Queens, Catherine and Mary of Medici—in
the midst of her noble family, the d'Angennes,

—in so many ways remarkable ; he saw her visited by Madame la Princesse, by Mademoiselle de Bourbon, who afterwards became the Duchesse de Longueville, and by the heroes of Rocroy ; and he met at her house the Duchesse d'Aiguillon, Vicomtesse d'Auchy, Madame de Sablé, Mademoiselle de Scudéry, Madame de Sévigné, Voiture, and that untamed lioness Mademoiselle Paulet, Vauglas, Malherbe, Racan, the two Corneilles, Mairet, Bensserade, Chapelain, Godeau, Huet, Menage, Gombauld, and, in short, everybody of note." No more favourable place for studying the fashionable society of the seventeenth century could have been found than this great Parisian house, so Tallemant des Réaux set to work to make the most of his opportunities, to keep his eyes and ears ever open, and to put upon paper whatever he saw or heard of interest. He collected there numerous stories of Cardinal Richelieu, Ninon de l'Enclos, and Marion de l'Orme ; he wrote down the anecdotes he had been told or the impressions he had obtained at the Marquise de Sévigné's, at Mademoiselle de Scudéry's, at the Comtesse de Maure's, or at Madame de Choisy's ; he tellingly described financial circles and that rich middle-class world whence he himself had sprung ; and, since he was writing merely for his own eyes and those of intimate friends, he snatched away—not, perhaps, without secret joy—the veil which thinly masked the failings of the aristocracy. It was some seven years after purchasing the Château of Réaux that he began to compile these reminiscences, which, when they were published for the first time in 1833, under the title of *Les Historiettes*, were universally pronounced to throw a most interesting and valuable light on the men, women, and morals of the seventeenth century. That many and many a hundred pages of these most fascinating memoirs were written at Réaux there cannot be the slightest doubt, and if for that reason only the place is well worthy of a pilgrimage. Tallemant des Réaux may himself be a somewhat shadowy figure, but his writings (the MS. of which was, I believe, found at the château) constitute such a collection of human documents that one naturally feels drawn towards the scene of their conception.

The next owner of the Château of Réaux was Louis Taboureau, Lord of Louy, councillor and secretary to the King, and on his death in Paris on May 30, 1746, it

passed to descendants, who, during the reign
of Louis XVI, built the wing to the left of
the entrance.   After remaining in the possession of this family for a very long time, it
was finally purchased, some ten or twelve years
ago, by its present owner, M. Julien Barois.

What little restoration the château needed
having been done about the year 1850,
M. Barois found the buildings in an excellent
state of preservation, and in that condition they
still remain.   He believes, however, that the
house was at one time much larger than it
is at present.   Near the moat—once crossed
by a drawbridge—and adjoining the tower
to the right of the entrance are the remains
of a wall, which in all probability belonged
to a building destroyed during an attack
on the château ;—and that it was actually
attacked is clearly proved by the bullet marks
to be seen here and there on its massive,
mellow walls.   But "what the eye does not
see the heart does not grieve over," and we
were, therefore, quite content with the
beauties which Réaux could offer us.   Viewed
from some parts of the grounds, it made a
most pretty picture, especially when the foreground was the tranquil, leaf-covered waters
of the moat.   We admired, too, the fine

PAINTED MANTELPIECE AT THE CHÂTEAU DE RÉAUX

FRANCIS I MANTELPIECE AT RÉAUX

Renaissance doorway leading from the back of the château to the main staircase, and, before visiting the interior, gave more than a passing glance at the Renaissance dormer-windows and the beautiful little lead figures of armoured knights, holding spears, which gallantly surmount the towers.

The drawing-room, which has a painted ceiling of great beauty, contains a Francis I mantelpiece in dark oak, a good example of modern wood-carving by the same artist whom the Marquis de Biencourt commissioned to ornament the bookcases and panelling in the library at the Château of Azay-le-Rideau. As regards decoration—and I may add that on the walls are many valuable family portraits—this is the most important room of the house. But the other rooms are in their way equally interesting, as, for instance, the quaint, cosy bedrooms, with their alcoves and ancient doors, provided with holes through which the cat could pass when tired of the company of the occupants ; and a certain little room, with painted fireplace, ceiling, and walls, situated at the very top of one of the towers. We reached this charming room by means of a narrow stone staircase, the handrail of which, similar to one we afterwards saw at Azay, is cut out of the stone,—a staircase so narrow that, as we squeezed ourselves up its winding steps, we wondered how any furniture could ever have been taken up it.   But perhaps it was never seriously intended to be anything else than a room for temporary occupation,—a sort of look-out over the surrounding country when the enemy was on the march.   Certainly a better point of vantage could not have been chosen, for the view from its windows extends as far as Saumur, whose grim castle, standing on a hill, can be distinctly seen on a fine day.

The sight of Saumur, gray and dim in the distance, reminded us that we must once more take to the road, and so, after making our adieus to our hosts, we started off to cover the ten miles which were to complete our journey down the Loire.

CHAPTER VII

AT SAUMUR AND MONTREUIL-BELLAY

THE traveller who has plenty of time at his disposal can easily spend a couple of agreeable days at Saumur. He might visit its several ancient churches, and profitably meditate on its religious vicissitudes, from the material effects of which it has never wholly recovered even to this day, though it is a long cry back to the period when, prior to the Revocation of the Edict of Nantes and the emigration of the Protestants, it was a large and prosperous Calvinistic town. He might see the sixteenth century Hôtel de Ville, with its library and natural history collections,—all a little dusty and neglected, as things are wont to be in the provinces. He might, on his way to the castle, explore the narrow, picturesque streets at the base of the hill which commands the valleys of the Loire and the Thouet, in search of old buildings, such

as the house in which Madame Dacier, the
translator of Homer and Aristophanes, was
born in 1651. He might, if of a military
turn of mind, inspect the cavalry school and
pass judgment on the horsemanship of French
officers. And, finally, he might even learn
how the renowned white wines of the district
are made to imitate champagne in everything
save lightness and delicacy of flavour. In our
case, however, the thought that we had as
yet seen barely half of what we had come to
Touraine to see, made us feel that we could
not afford to devote more than half a day
to Saumur, with the result that the major
part of its attractions had to be accepted
on hearsay from the lips of a loquacious
old gentleman whom we chanced to meet
at the hotel. Whether his knowledge of
archæology was as sound as his taste for
vin blanc mousseux was pronounced, I am not
quite certain; but we agreed to give him
the benefit of the doubt.

The shortness of our stay naturally led to a
mere cursory inspection of some of the antiquities of Saumur. The castle was the only
building we saw at all thoroughly, and
consequently it is the only one on which I
have any right to speak. Turning up one of

THE CASTLE OF SAUMUR

the small streets facing the Quai de Limoges, a very steep and circuitous path, winding through hillside gardens, brought us to the entrance, where we found the unavoidable guide waiting to receive us. The rôle he took, however, was a very unobtrusive one, consisting as it did in leading us from dungeon to dungeon, and from turret to turret, almost without a word of comment. He allowed us to linger as long as we pleased ; he did not presume to enter into our conversation. It was a pleasant change to feel that one had no competitor when recounting the history— such as it is—of the castle.

Geoffrey Martel, the son of Fulk the Black, began to build it in the eleventh century, but, like most mediæval fortresses, it was not completed until later,—until the thirteenth and fourteenth centuries. Battles were waged beneath its precipitous enceinte ; it was won now by one, now by another fierce leader. Centuries of continued strife naturally brought in their train numerous changes in its architecture. It originally consisted of four large wings, but one of these has entirely disappeared, leaving a central courtyard open to the valley of the Loire. This courtyard contains the most decorative portions of one

of the most undecorative of the castles of
Touraine : the sculptured exterior of a staircase, with niches which are said to have once
held statues, and, over a doorway, a bas-
relief, representing two wrestlers—presumably
Gauls—covered with long hair. The latter
work has every appearance of being exceedingly ancient, and it is probably even older
than the castle itself. In the courtyard, also,
stands a curious construction pierced with
openings and with a domed roof. This gave
air, rather than light, to a dark, subterranean
room in which the lord of the castle tried his
prisoners ; and as to the methods he employed
to obtain evidence, we could form a very
good idea in the glimmer of the guide's
lantern. At one end of the chamber there
is a sort of platform on which the lord and
his advisers sat in judgment, and beneath this
can still be seen part of the apparatus which
was used to drag confession from their
enemies. Many a time must that courtyard have rung with the screams of tortured
men.

Grimness is the distinctive note of the
Castle of Saumur. When its " memories "
are not actually sinister, they are never very
agreeable. You cannot think of it as a resi-

COURTYARD OF THE CASTLE OF SAUMUR

dence for any one except a mediæval warrior, continually on the alert ; and it is for that reason, I suppose, that it has never been anything else than a fortress, a prison, or a barracks. Descending to its dungeons, it was clear from the names and dates and pathetic words scratched on the walls to what purpose the castle had been put as far back as the days of Nicolas Foucquet, who spent part of his long imprisonment there. Napoleon I, too, used it as a prison. After that it became a barracks,—a further step in its degradation. Here and there in its interior we could trace the remains of former decoration, but the rooms have been so cut up and mutilated that it was utterly impossible to reconstitute their ancient disposition. The pleasantest part of our visit came when we ascended to the top of one of the towers, whence we obtained, as the day was favourable, a perfect view in all directions, to Chinon and Bourgueil in the east, and even as far as Angers, whose cathedral spires gleamed in the north-west.

The pleasure we had experienced in travelling along the banks of the Loire had made us decide to follow the other rivers of Touraine, whenever possible, in a similar

manner ; and we should much have liked, on
leaving Saumur, to have explored the meandering course of the Thouet, which flows
into the Loire a little below that town.   But
practical difficulties stood in the way of such
a journey, so we took the direct road to
Montreuil-Bellay, the point on the pretty
little tributary where we were to see another
château.

As we arrived within sight of its massive
towers, rising from amidst the trees on the
summit of a hillock, I could not help mentally
commenting on the contrast it formed to the
severity and bareness of the Castle of Saumur.
Indeed, we had as yet seen no more
picturesque setting for a country residence.
The Thouet, elsewhere a narrow stream,
widens out at Montreuil - Bellay into a
broad basin, divided into four branches by
a number of islets, thickly wooded and
covered with vegetation to the water's edge.
It abounds with countless little sedgy back-
waters, begemmed in summer with white and
yellow water-lilies, and, like the islets themselves, alive with birds.   It possesses two
bridges, one dating from the Middle Ages, the
other from 1811 ; and at the foot of the
latter — completing the delightful picture

which can be seen from the castle's battlements—stands an ancient mill.

In tracing the origin of Montreuil-Bellay
and its château one can go very far back in
history. That the district was inhabited in
prehistoric times has been shown by the
discovery of flint implements, and also by the
existence, near the little town, of prehistoric
monuments. A Gallo-Roman village is said
to have stood on the same site, though no
conclusive proof of this has yet been brought
forward. Later a feudal castle, surrounded by
the dwellings of villains and serfs, was built
on the hill above the Thouet ; and this early
fortress is commonly believed to have fallen
into the hands of Fulk the Black, who gave
it in fief, about the year 1025, to a supporter
named Berlay or Bellay, the brother-in-law of
the man whom he had conquered. Bellay
and his descendants, hoping to be able to
dispense with the authority of the counts of
Anjou, fortified the castle, whereupon Fulk v
set out against them, and, in 1124, captured
their stronghold. The ambition of another
member of the same family, Giraud II, was
similarly shattered twenty-six years later,
when Geoffrey Plantagenet laid siege to the
castle, which he did not capture, however,

until 1151, just a year from the time his troops had first encamped beneath its solid walls.

The next family to own the feudal castle of Montreuil-Bellay was that of the House of Melun, and with one of its descendants, Guillaume IV, Count of Tancarville, we come to the building of the present château. Early in the fifteenth century he constructed the Château-Vieil, in addition to a strong wall around the town, a wall the remains of which still exist, and which you must certainly see before leaving the district. The Harcourts, a Normandy family which held a position in the front rank of the French nobility, were the owners at the end of the fifteenth and the beginning of the sixteenth centuries. They built the Château-Neuf and completed the Collegiate Church, which stands in the château grounds. The domain then passed to the House of Dunois, or Orleans-Longue-ville.

During the Wars of Religion, Montreuil-Bellay was occupied by the Huguenots' army, Henry of Navarre having captured it in 1589 whilst marching against Henry III. In 1622 the château was sold to Marshal de la Meilleraye, from whose hands it

A VIEW OF THE TOWERS OF MONTREUIL-BELLAY

passed to the House of Brissac, which possessed it until 1756, the date at which it was again sold, this time to the Duc de la Trémoille.

Confiscated during the Revolution, it was captured from General Saloman, on the night of June 8, 1793, by the royalists of the Vendée, but was retaken shortly afterwards by the Republicans, who for nearly a year used it as a prison for several hundred women whom the Committee of Public Safety had had arrested as *suspectes*. On the 6th of Messidor, Year IV, it was sold as national property to a merchant named Augustin Glaçon. But on the 25th of Brumaire, Year V, the sale was annulled, and the Trémoïlle family re-entered into possession, at first provisionally and then definitely. It was once more, and for the last time, sold on April 15, 1822. The new owner, M. Niveleau, bequeathed it to his son, M. Adrien Niveleau, who left it to his sister, Baronne Millin de Grandmaison, who in turn, in 1890, left it to her grand-nephew, the present owner, Baron Georges Millin de Grandmaison, the grandson of Marshal Lobau.

After so stormy a period as the Revolution, the Château of Montreuil-Bellay was naturally

in great need of restoration.   M. Niveleau *père*
did much to make it habitable, but Madame
de Grandmaison thought that something more
than mere absolutely necessary repairs was
due to a house which had given hospitality
to such illustrious people as Louis VIII,
Charles VII, Dunois, Louis XI, Charles VIII,
Duplessis-Mornay, Henry IV, Louis XIII, the
Duchesse de Longueville, and Anne of Austria.
So she commissioned M. Joly-Leterme, an
architect of Saumur who had already restored
public buildings in that town, to do his
utmost to restore its exterior and its interior
to the state it was in during its palmiest days.
Most zealously did he carry out his work ;
and if he is to be in any way criticised it is
for being over-zealous as regards the decoration
of the château rooms, some of which are
perhaps a little too brilliant in their colouring.

The entrance to the château is between the
towers of the Château-Vieil, once protected by
a drawbridge.   Passing into the *Cour d'honneur*,
which forms a large terrace overlooking the
garden and river, you see to the left the
Château-Neuf and, adjoining, in an angle of
the castle's enceinte, a curious little building
with four round towers and conical slate roofs.

THE MEDIÆVAL KITCHEN AT MONTREUIL-BELLAY

THE TOP OF THE "ESCALIER D'HONNEUR" AT
MONTREUIL-BELLAY

MONTREUIL-BELLAY: THE CHÂTEAU NEUF

This is known as the Petit Château, and it dates from the fifteenth century. It was probably used by some of the canons who officiated in the Collegiate Church; and as these dignitaries were quite as fond of good living as their master the Lord of Montreuil-Bellay, what more natural than that the kitchen of the castle should be next door to them? Like many mediæval buildings used for a similar purpose, this kitchen is separate from the château proper; but, instead of being round or polygonal, as is usually the case, it is square. It possesses two fireplaces, which are still in use; a third, and a double one, was in the centre, but this has been modified, though the central brick chimney, from which huge spits were once suspended for the roasting of quarters of oxen, still remains. Alterations have also been made to the doors and windows. But in spite of these modifications the building does not lose any of its interest; it is, indeed, in the opinion of Viollet-le-Duc, who has devoted many lines to it in his *Dictionnaire d'Architecture*, one of the most remarkable kitchens in France.

In visiting the Château-Neuf, we entered by a door in its large octagonal tower, which contains the main staircase, the steps of which, alternately white and gray, are so gentle that, to use the words of one who described the castle in the eighteenth century, "a horse could easily mount to the third-floor, forty feet from the ground." At the top of this *escalier d'honneur* is a beautiful fan vaulting, with bosses bearing the coloured escutcheons of the various families who have owned the château.

Apart from the Château of Langeais, I cannot think of any private residence in Touraine where you can see such fine rooms as those at Montreuil-Bellay. The colouring may, as I have already said, be slightly overdone, but there are so many other features in their favour that that is soon forgiven and forgotten. The chimney-pieces are in the purest Flamboyant style; the prismatic mullioned windows have recesses of extraordinary depth; and the decorated ceilings, with their huge beams, are so unique that they alone would easily provide matter for a special study. I spent nearly an hour examining these ceilings, and even then I had not exhausted all that they had to show. In their case I imagine that the hand of the restorer played but a minor part;

though I was interested not so much by their design and colour as by the extremely curious mediæval grotesques which are carved on the main beams in the dining-room, in the Salle de Longueville, in the Chambre de la Trémoïlle, and in other rooms. Placed sometimes at the ends, sometimes in the centre, these strange carvings produce a weird impression on the onlooker, carrying him back to the days when almost anything was licensed in art. The artist who executed them had evidently no fear of shocking the sensibilities of the inhabitants of the château, presuming that he did not receive explicit instructions to give free rein to his imagination. In one corner he has carved the head of a giant in the act of swallowing a nude woman ; in another, the squat figure of an animal, to be seen nowhere in nature ; in a third place, the body of a crouching dog with the head of a nun ; and in a fourth, a grinning dwarf whose attitude is such as to preclude description. Many of them, in fact, have to be placed in this last category. You cannot imagine how realistic they are until you have seen them, and their realism is further heightened by the addition of colour. As regards the furnishing of the

rooms, the Château of Montreuil-Bellay is
a perfect museum. The countless works of
art to be seen on all sides include carved
Renaissance sideboards and beds, Boule
cabinets, tables inlaid with tortoise-shell,
Empire chairs, seventeenth and eighteenth
century clocks, Venetian mirrors, Nevers,
Rouen, and Italian china, suits of armour
and ancient weapons, seventeenth and
eighteenth century andirons, firebacks bearing
the arms of great families, ancient locks and
keys, and a large number of similar objects
in wrought-iron. The tapestries deserve
mention by themselves. There are two
Brussels panels of the sixteenth century:
one, which is incomplete, representing the
departure of Paulus Æmilius for Greece;
the other, which bears the words *Perseus
thesauros suos navi committit et frustra cogitans
fugam in templo se adscondit*, showing Perseus
putting his treasures in a place of safety.
Gobelins and Beauvais tapestries of the
eighteenth century, depicting such games as
Blind Man's Buff and Hot Cockles, are in
the dining-room; whilst in other rooms
are various others, including a series of
Aubusson. The pictures, we were told, are
less important than the tapestries, so, as our

THE TRÉMOÏLLE BEDROOM AT MONTREUIL-BELLAY

time was growing short, we forewent these and hurried off to the oratory, a little room which, though its painted walls and its vaulted, painted ceiling have lost much of their original richness and harmony, is still not without beauty.

The garden, owing to the necessarily cramped space within the castle walls and its position on the slope of a hill, is not a feature of Montreuil-Bellay ; consequently, we did no more than pass through it by a gently sloping path which descends the hillside and leads to the public road on the bank of the river. Following this road, which replaced the rampart that once skirted the main branch of the stream, we soon came to one of the existing walls, terminated by a round tower at the water's edge and pierced by a semicircular doorway, bearing the date April 30, 1669. We passed through,— and not far from there found our boatman. I can assure you that there is no more fitting way of concluding a visit to Montreuil-Bellay than by making an excursion on the river, for it enables you to examine the remains of the fifteenth century bridge which crossed the stream at this point of its course, to obtain certain views of the château which cannot be had from any other position, and—what is perhaps even more important, after seeing so much—to rest the eye in the green and shady nooks and corners of the islands of the Thouet.

CHAPTER VIII

ALONG THE VIENNE: TO CHINON

IF, whilst in Touraine, you are anywhere within a reasonable distance of Fontevrault, by all means make a point of visiting it, since to neglect to do so is one of those omissions which afterwards weigh heavily on a traveller's conscience. In our case, this ancient little town happened to lie on the direct route from Montreuil-Bellay to the mouth of the Vienne; but had it been necessary to go out of our way to see it, we should not have hesitated to make the detour. Nay, after seeing its antiquities, the celebrity of which had long aroused our curiosity, I should not have considered we had come too far had we made a special journey of a hundred kilometres.

Fontevrault is peculiarly interesting to English people. Henry II of England, his wife Eleonora of Guyenne, Richard Cœur

de Lion, and John's wife, Isabella of
Angoulême, were buried in its famous abbey ;
and although their graves, with those of
many other royal personages, were desecrated
at the time of the Revolution, the statues
which covered them can still be seen in one
of the transepts of the abbey church. The
statue of Isabella, who is represented holding
an open book in her hands, is of oak ; the
other effigies are of soft calcareous stone ;
and all are coloured, though not with the
colours which enhanced their beauty in the
twelfth century.

The abbey, which was founded about the
end of the eleventh century by Robert of
Arbrissel, a Breton priest of great fame as
a preacher and ascetic, was regarded with
particular favour by royalty, no fewer than
fourteen of the abbesses who succeeded
Petronella de Craon-Chemillé, the first to
hold the office, being princesses. And until
its suppression in 1793 it continued to be
the usual place to which young ladies of
the blood royal of France were sent for
education.

In another respect the order of Fontevrault
was equally noteworthy ; it was, indeed,
unique in so far as it consisted of both

nuns and monks, under the sole authority of an abbess.

How beautiful their abbey must have been at one time of its history may be judged by what remains of its architectural features after more than a century of ill-treatment. The work of mutilation begun by the revolutionaries of 1793 was continued when the fine old abbey was turned, early in the nineteenth century, into a convict prison,—a degrading use to which we were surprised to find it continues to be put. But, in spite of the irreparable damage which was done up to as late as 1816, and which the authorities are now seeking to repair by tardy restoration, the buildings are still exceedingly fine specimens of the architecture of the twelfth and sixteenth centuries.

In addition to seeing the church, we paid an only too brief visit, under the guidance of a warder, to the cloisters and the chapter house. The southern ambulatory, which skirts the refectory, dates from the early years of the sixteenth century, but the three other galleries were not built until 1540, if not until as late as 1560. The tiling, which you cannot fail to notice just before entering the chapter house, is also sixteenth century work, as well as the magnificently carved doorway and the mural paintings—unfortunately in very poor condition—by Thomas Pot and other artists of the Renaissance.

Two other churches, both of the twelfth century, were connected with the Abbey of Fontevrault: the Church of St. Lazarus, now used as an infirmary, and the Church of St. Benedict. But the prison regulations forbid either these or a curious building of the same period, which we chanced to catch a glimpse of on leaving, to be visited. Inspection of the former we felt we could easily forgo, but it was hard to have to drag ourselves away without seeing the interior of the latter, of which we had read an account in Viollet-le-Duc's great dictionary. The Tour d'Evrault, as it is called, is a building of three storeys: the first an octagon, the second a square, and the third an octagon; and these are surmounted by a sort of pyramidal structure. For a long time it was supposed to have been used as a chapel, but it is now known to have been the abbey kitchen. Comparison with the kitchens of Montreuil-

Bellay and Moulin would have been instructive. We found consolation for this deprivation in the thirteenth century chapel of St. Catherine, now a private house facing an avenue of lime trees, and in the parish church of St. Michel, noteworthy for the extremely picturesque wooden construction surrounding it, as well as for an altar in gilded wood, dating from 1621, and other art treasures which were once in the neighbouring abbey.

It was not long, after leaving Fontevrault, before we renewed acquaintance with our old friend the Loire. There, at the turning of the road leading to Chinon, the ancient town of Montsoreau, an incident in whose history inspired Alexandre Dumas with a heroine and a title for one of his novels, tempted us to tarry. But neither its churches nor its fifteenth century château had power to do more than slightly slacken our pace as we swept along towards the more attractive little town of Candès, then almost within sight.

Candès is a Gallic name meaning "confluent," and, as you rightly suppose, it is situated at the point where the Loire and the Vienne join forces. The meeting

of the rivers, which can best be viewed
from the terraced garden of a gentleman's
house on the slope of the hill above the
narrow, winding streets of the town, helps,
with the aid of distant pastures and browsing
cattle, to form a most beautiful picture,
above all towards the close of evening,
when the wide expanse of water, as still
as a lake, is rich in deep, subtle reflections.
This not-to-be-forgotten view will be found
to be a very pleasant afterpiece to your
visit to the church of St. Martin, which
was built in the twelfth and fourteenth
centuries, and the square, machicolated
towers of which are on a level with this
terrace.

To find so important a church as that
of St. Martin in so small a place as Candès
is an anomaly which rarely fails to strike
those who pass that way. It is, indeed,
a cathedral in miniature, resembling, in
some respects, that of Poitiers. A finer
proportioned building you will not meet
anywhere, and such graceful, slender pillars
as those which rise to its beautiful vaulted
roof you will see only in the choicest
examples of ecclesiastical architecture. The
decoration, too, is remarkable, for its

sculpture is not only original in its character and abundant but also coloured. The
porch, which bears the name of St. Michel,
is likewise an exquisite piece of carving,
notwithstanding the mutilation which its
statues have undergone ; and, in addition,
I would have you notice how particularly
elegant is the manner in which the ribs of
the vaulted roof spread out from the slender
central column which supports it.

The saint to whom this beautiful church
is dedicated founded a monastery at Candès,
and on the site of a lateral apse, a little
older than the church itself, stood the cell
in which he died about the year 400.
This portion of the edifice has been entirely
rebuilt, and a modern stained glass window
tells how St. Martin's body was removed
at night-time by his followers and taken
up the Loire for burial at Tours.

The country between Candès and Chinon
is of a wilder character than that along
the banks of the Loire, and, comparing
river with river, the Vienne is the more
ruggedly picturesque. As you pass along
the road, bordered now with poplars, now
with walnut trees, from whose fruit the
inhabitants of the district obtain an oil

which they prefer to that of the olive,
the exuberance of Nature is on all sides
apparent. You feel that you are now in the
true Touraine,—the Touraine of Rabelais.
It is a country of fruit-ladened orchards,
of vineyards productive of much red wine,
and of rich pasture-land; a country peopled
by a genial, joke-loving, full-blooded population, primitive in their manners and customs
and perhaps a little lax in their morals.
You can picture it, without being far
wrong, as a pale reflection of the *Heroic
Deeds and Sayings of the Good Pantagruel*,
which, as is only natural, contains many
allusions to Chinon and places in the
district through which you are passing.
For the author of that immortal book was
a man of these parts, and may be regarded
as typifying both his age and his birthplace. Some authorities say that he was
born at Chinon, about the year 1483;
others that he first saw the light on the
estate of La Devinière, near La Roche-
Clermault; and it is known for certain
that he began his studies in the Benedictine
Abbey of Seuilly, barely a mile from the
latter place. Whilst at St. Germain-sur-
Vienne, where we stopped the night, in

THE CHÂTEAU DE PETIT-THOUARS

DINING-ROOM AT THE CHÂTEAU DE PETIT-THOUARS

order to be able to keep an appointment
at the neighbouring Château of Petit
Thouars, we had an opportunity of con-
firming our impression as to Rabelais'
writings and the characteristics of the
present-day population of the Rabelais
country. One of the most primitive of
village inns was our quarters; our companions were the sons and daughters of the
soil; and such conditions as those are in-
dispensable if you would learn anything
of the intimate side of a people's life and
mentality. At the same time we saw the
Vienne under some of its most pleasing
aspects. At this part of its course, a few
miles from Candès, it is a slow-moving,
majestic river bordered with willows and
poplars, and dotted here and there with
thickly wooded islands. Seen in the gray
light of early morning or during a sunset,
when the fishermen's boats, with their
hanging nets, are moored in mid-stream,
and the wooded banks stand out against
a roseate sky, shading into a delicate green,
it is equally fascinating, and, as my companion, who is an artist, remarked, is
suggestive of countless pictures.

The Château of Petit Thouars, which

stands above St. Germain, on the summit of
the range of hills overlooking the valley of
the Vienne, was built in 1440, at the time
when Charles VII was holding his frivolous
Court at the Castle of Chinon. According
to certain documents, it is supposed to have
been constructed by one of the King's
ministers, the Sire de la Trémouïlle, who
was then the owner of the Château of
Thouars, in the Department of Deux-Sèvres.
After passing through the hands of various
owners, it was acquired in 1610 by the
Aubert de St. Georges family, the elder
branch of which still possesses it. The
present owner is M. Georges Aubert de St.
Georges, Comte du Petit Thouars.

Its architecture, as has so often happened
in the case of old buildings, has undergone
many changes, in accordance with the varying
tastes of successive occupants, and its style is
now that of the period of Louis XII. The
oldest and best preserved part of the château
is an interior courtyard, where, on the
windows of a tower, can be seen some exceedingly old sculpture. The interior of this
tower consists of a winding stone staircase,
which, like the principal façade and other
parts of the building, has been recently

restored.   In the garden stands a picturesque
circular dovecote of huge dimensions,—the
only one we saw in Touraine.

The interior of Petit Thouars, though it
does not call for a lengthy description, contains several things of considerable interest to
the connoisseur.   In the drawing-room is a
rather fine mantelpiece, bearing the arms of
the Aubert de St. Georges family ; but your
attention will soon be diverted from this to
the pictures on the walls.   These are reduced
copies of some of the works, representing the
principal events in the life of Marie de' Medici,
which Rubens painted for that Queen between
1621 and 1625, and which, until they were
removed to the Louvre, under the Second
Empire, were in a gallery, adjoining her
bedroom, in the Luxembourg Palace.   They
were the work of one of the numerous skilful
pupils whom the celebrated painter had in
his studio at Antwerp, and they were specially
executed for the Château of Petit Thouars,
where they have remained ever since the
seventeenth century.   On the dining-room
walls are a number of family portraits, including two ancestors of M. Georges Aubert
de St. Georges who were military governors
of the castle and district of Saumur.   The

painted ceilings of these two rooms were
repainted at the time of the last restoration
of the château, and their designs recall certain
of those on the ceilings at the Castle of Blois.

Our entry into Chinon was made on just
such a day as that on which I would have
you see this delightful old town and its
magnificent ruined castle. It was a glorious
sunny August morning, hours before the
summer heat had become inconvenient. The
sky was a deep Italian blue, with white fleecy
clouds, snow-white under the sun, floating
slowly along as far as the horizon. The air
had that perfect clarity which makes all but
the most distant objects seem quite near at
hand. The three distinct fortresses of which
the castle is composed — the Château de
Saint Georges, the Château du Milieu, and
the Château du Coudray, stretching in a line
from east to west on the steep hill on whose
side and base the houses nestle, tier upon
tier — were particularly illusive in their
apparent nearness, as we found on climbing
the winding streets which lead to the entrance.
Long though the climb was, however, it was
anything but wearisome, for our attention
was continually being directed to some fresh
object of curiosity : at one time to an old

THE CASTLE OF CHINON

A VIEW OF CHINON FROM THE CASTLE

house with carved wooden front and doorway; at another, to a charming little
sculptured window, or ancient piece of
wrought-iron work; and again, to picturesque
white-washed cottages, festooned with vines,
in streets where the brilliant sunshine and
deep sharp-edged shadows gave one the impression of being under a southern sky.

As we reached the top of the hill and stood
resting on a bridge preceding the Pavillon de
l'Horloge, where we had been told to ring
for entrance, and whose tower, over a hundred
feet in height, contains a clock which is said
to have struck the hours for close upon four
centuries, I was reminded by the view of the
lines quoted by Pantagruel in that chapter
of his *Faicts et Dicts Heroiques*, in which it is
claimed that Chinon (*Caino*) was built by Cain
and is, therefore, " the oldest city in the world."

> "Chinon,
> Little town,
> Great renown,
> On old stone
> Long has stood;
> There's the Vienne, if you look down;
> If you look up, there's the wood."

The description still holds good, and it is likely
to do so until the end of time. As the cluster
of gray, irregular-roofed houses lying im-

mediately beneath our feet clearly showed,
Chinon is ever the little town it was in
Rabelais' day. It has maintained its reputation, too, in comparison with other celebrated
old towns of France, — a reputation un-
paralleled as regards picturesqueness, whatever
its position may be from the point of view of
history. In tracing its story, one need go no
farther back than Roman times, when it was
an important military centre, connected by
splendid roads with other strategical points of
Touraine. Early Christian saints chose it as
a place for the foundation of churches and a
monastery. A little later, about 500, when
Clovis was preparing to unite his conquests
from the Loire to the Pyrenees, he made it
one of his principal fortresses : and thus set
an example which was to be followed down
the centuries by the counts of Touraine, by
Geoffrey Martel, by Henry II of England,
by Charles VII, and by Louis XI. To at least
one of these princes, Chinon was, however,
something more than a mere stronghold. To
Henry II it was his favourite residence on the
Continent, and you can quite understand the
reason why, if you consider what a matchless
view he had from his castle windows : here,
in the foreground, the gray little town ;

there, the Vienne, sparkling in the sunlight for mile upon mile, mirroring the trees on its banks and the clouds in the sky; and beyond, the fresh green wooded country, stretching to a hazy horizon.

Our visit to the castle was made doubly enjoyable by the fact that we were accompanied by a guide who left us plenty of time to indulge in historical recollections. He was a small boy of seven, with neither hat nor coat, and with stockingless legs as brown as mahogany. In the most delightful, unceremonious way he led us from dismantled room to crumbling bastion, and from tower to dungeon, repeating the history of each place in his delightfully innocent infantile manner. Then, when he had repeated his well-learnt lesson, he would run away to climb a ruined battlement, where, in an almost inaccessible crevice, he had espied some wild pinks, or to chase a butterfly which had fluttered past us in the tangled garden into which the space between the castle walls has been converted. Had we not perceived that he was as sure-footed as a chamois we should more than once have feared to see him fall headlong into the moats beneath our feet.

Chinon, like Fontevrault, will ever be interesting to English people on King Henry's account, little estimable though he was as husband and father. In addition to his frequent sojourns at the castle, he died there in 1189, on hearing from the French ambassadors that his favourite son John had joined his brothers in their revolt against him. This dramatic event occurred in that part of the castle called the Grand-Logis, where Henry was then lying sick and bedridden. "On hearing his son's name," runs the record, "he was seized with a sort of convulsive movement, sat up in bed, and, gazing around with searching and haggard eyes, exclaimed, 'Can it be true that John, my heart, the son of my choice, him whom I have doted on more than all the rest, and my love for whom has brought on me all my woes, has fallen away from me?' They replied that it was even so; that nothing could be more true. 'Well, then,' he said, falling back on his bed, and turning his face to the wall, 'henceforward let all go on as it may; I no longer care for myself nor for the world.'" Another famous interview, that between Jeanne Darc and Charles VII, and which heralded the downfall of English rule in France, took place in that

THE CHÂTEAU DE COULAINE

same room some two and a half centuries later.
Amidst the light of torches and a brilliant
assembly of nobles, the Maid entered "like a
poor little shepherdess" and singled out the
King from amongst the crowd of courtiers
with whom he had purposely mingled, thus
taking the first definite step towards prevailing
upon him to throw off his lethargy and raise
the siege of Orleans.   During her five weeks'
residence at the castle she occupied a still
existing tower of the Château du Coudray.
These are the two principal historical pictures
which the Castle of Chinon summons to the
mind.   But it will suggest a host of other
minor events and characters which have
passed across the stage of history, and among
them none more noteworthy than the introduction of Agnes Sorel—*la belle des belles*—to
the Court of Charles VII.   When one of the
Queen's maids-of-honour she had, of course,
her appointed apartment ; but after she had
won Charles' entire affection she was provided
with a house in the neighbourhood, and the
King, in order to be able to visit her in secret,
connected it with the castle by means of a
subterranean passage.

Before leaving Chinon and district for the
southern portion of Touraine we made an

14

excursion of a few miles to Beaumont-en-
Véron, a little removed from the banks of the
Vienne, to see the pretty little Château of
Coulaine, and, unless you are very pressed
for time, you may be recommended to do
the same. It was built in 1470 by Jean
Garguesalle, *premier écuyer* to Louis XI and
Governor of Chinon. About the middle of
the sixteenth century it was owned by Henri
de Craon, who took part, in 1559, in the
reform of the Customs of Touraine, and whose
son Claude, born at the château in 1556,
became a celebrated Greek scholar. The
Dowager Baroness de Coulaine de Clock, a
descendant of the Garguesalle family, is the
present owner. Its graceful façade consists of
a slender octagonal tower, containing a staircase, flanked by two wings, each terminated
by a smaller round tower,—a façade decorated
with foliage, mediæval figures, and over each
pair of windows a swan and the head of a
stag. Its most elaborate piece of sculpture is
that of the doorway, on which are the arms of
the Coulaine family and their motto: "Va
ferme à l'assault qui sit à la prise."

CHAPTER IX

AT LE GRAND PRESSIGNY AND LA GUERCHE

TO a large number of the many thousands of people who annually visit Touraine some of the finer features of the scenery of the ancient province remain unknown. As a rule, tourists travel in the districts of the Loire and the Indre ; they follow, perhaps, a part of the course of the Vienne ; and they touch, say, at two or three points on the Cher where there are famous country houses ; but they leave unseen, since they go no farther south than Loches, the more exhilarating landscapes of that valley of the river Creuse whose beauties —almost unknown in France some half a century ago—have been so glowingly described by George Sand. On only one plea is this omission pardonable, — that of shortness of time, an obstacle to travel which is further increased in this, as in other parts of France, by an execrable train service. And here let me point out that the only way of seeing Touraine thoroughly is to travel by motor-car or on a cycle. Masters of the open road and with a reasonable amount of time at your disposal, there can be no excuse for not visiting the gorges of the Creuse.

"The river," says the Abbé Chevalier in his *Promenades Pittoresque en Touraine*,— "the river, sometimes calm and peaceful in the deep basins formed by the natural irregularities of the ground, each a lower level than the other, sometimes rushing along, amidst foam, and with a roar, down the steep slopes over which it must pass at point after point, meanders capriciously from one side of the valley to the other, but with a preference for skirting the western side. Here, the bare hillside drops perpendicularly into the water ; there, it is a cliff all pierced with caverns, which must at one time have been the dwellings of men of primitive ages ; farther on, it becomes less wild and is decked with pleasant verdure. The horizon, a slightly uneven line, is everywhere extensive. The landscape consists of animated undulating country opening up distance beyond distance."

This picturesque valley of gorges begins at Confolent, near Fresselines, where the Petite

Creuse joins the greater river, and can perhaps best be seen there, in the department of La Creuse ; but you can form a very good idea of its beauty without leaving the geographical area which you have chosen as a holiday ground, without going farther than La Guerche, where, apart from beautiful scenery, you will find a fine old château.

A splendid national road—such a one as is found anywhere in France, and which makes motoring and cycling in that country so enjoyable—leads from Chinon to this new district by way of St. Epain, Ste. Maure, La Celle St. Avant, La Haye-Descartes (a little town in which René Descartes, the philosopher, was born on March 31, 1596), and Le Grand Pressigny. From Ste. Maure to Le Grand Pressigny the country is one of poplars, and the nearer you approach the end of the first half of your journey to La Guerche the wilder and hillier it becomes. On reaching Le Grand Pressigny you should make a halt, in order to see the ruins of its castle, to hunt for implements of the Stone Age, and perhaps to stop a night (as we did) under the red-tiled roof of one of its primitive yet homely inns.

The principal feature of the castle, which crowns a hill overlooking the little town, is its keep, an imposing square tower, thirty yards high and more than seven yards broad, bearing the scars of a hundred battles, out of all of which it has come forth still stout and strong. Time has damaged it infinitely more than the hand of man. The most dilapidated part is the machicolated top, which was added at the end of the fourteenth century, the rest of the tower dating from about the middle of the twelfth. This keep was the centre, in the thirteenth and fourteenth centuries, of a complete system of defensive works, consisting of ramparts with turrets at the corners, moat, glacis, etc. ; but no trace of these remain. The existing ivy - covered enceinte, which was once strongly fortified, as you can see by the remains of its towers, was built to replace them at a later period, it is supposed at the beginning of the fifteenth century. Some hundred years later, the lord of the castle, finding that his stronghold was not particularly well adapted for the purpose of a residence, had a house built near at hand, and parts of this, now occupied by the gendarmery, are still standing.

LE GRAND PRESSIGNY: THE KEEP

THE CHÂTEAU DE LA GUERCHE

Apart from the castle, Le Grand Pressigny is interesting to archæologists on account of the large number of implements of the Stone Age which have been found there. The peasants of the district, some years ago, used to plough them up by thousands and wonder what they were. Not until the sixties was the importance of their discovery made known to the scientific world. A certain Dr. Léveillé had his attention drawn to these skilfully fashioned arrow - heads, spears, axes, and wedges; and he at once saw that only the hand of man could have produced them. Further inquiry brought to light the fact that they were to be found in equally large numbers in the four Communes of Chaumussay, Abilly, Barrou, and La Guerche,—a clear proof that Le Grand Pressigny and district formed an immense workshop for the production of these tools and weapons, and that for some now unknown reason it was abandoned with its entire stock-in-trade. The curé of Chaumussay has a fine collection of these flint implements, and he will be glad to show it to you, if you care to run over from Le Grand Pressigny—it is only five miles away—to see him.

On leaving Le Grand Pressigny for La Guerche, a winding departmental road mounts a steep hill, and on reaching the top you proceed through a country of small fir trees. Furze and heather border the way, a beautiful edging of yellow and purple which stretches out, in mingled patches, under the trees. This touch of colour comes to an end only too soon. The edge of the plateau is quickly reached, and then, with fruit trees on either hand, you rapidly descend to La Guerche and the valley of the Creuse.

The Château of La Guerche, which we visited before exploring the banks of the river, is not one of the show-places of Touraine. It is remarkable neither for its architecture, nor its sculpture, nor its gardens. You will look in vain in its rather neglected rooms for such superb tapestries or such rare pieces of furniture as are to be seen at Langeais, though it possesses two or three carved cabinets which few connoisseurs would scorn to place in their collections. And amongst its pictures you will find but a small number of works, if any, worthy of being compared with the masterpieces of Chenonceaux. Yet it is one of those places the recollection of which outlasts that of many another more renowned château. Its charm is that of the unrestored, untended building,—a charm than which, to certain minds, there is none more potent. If you are poetically inclined, you will be bound to appreciate its tangled, moss-grown court-yard, with its fountain-basin green with age. If you are a lover of the picturesque, you will be delighted with its situation on the beautiful Creuse, from whose stony bed its towers rise more than a hundred feet. If you like those houses which are enveloped in a spirit of romance, you will not regret having included it in your programme. Poetry, picturesqueness, and, above all, romance, — such are the characteristics of La Guerche.

An historian of the Châteaux of Touraine once said that La Guerche was " the mysterious boudoir of the fifteenth century." He could not have given it a more appropriate descrip-tion, for there is a love story inextricably bound up with its history, and authorities differ as to the way it should be told. That the château was built for a lady by Charles VII every one agrees, but as to who that lady was—Agnes Sorel or Antoinette de Maignelais

—they wholly disagree. M. Raoul de Croy, the owner of the château, is a firm believer, with others, that it was Agnes Sorel, and that La Guerche has every bit as much right to be regarded as a former home of the King's *amie par amour* as Cheillé, Champigny, or any other of her Touraine houses. He claims, moreover, not only to have located the very room in which she slept, a small bedroom with an alcove and a deeply recessed window which looks out on to the dark waters of the Creuse, but also to possess the tomb, covered with a very mutilated statue, which he says was erected to her memory in the eleventh century church at La Guerche. This tomb and statue you will see in a long corridor adjoining the bedroom. Unfortunately for these assertions, not one of those who have advanced them have ever brought forward any proof; they rest wholly on tradition; whereas the historians who hold that the château was built for the other lady are able, with the aid of documentary evidence, to make out a very strong case. Here are the facts, as given by M. Carré de Busserolle, the soundest authority one can consult in studying the archæology of the Indre-et-Loire.

THE BILLIARD-ROOM AT LA GUERCHE

CHÂTEAU DE LA GUERCHE: AGNES SOREL'S BEDROOM

The estate of La Guerche, on which there once stood an even older castle than the present château, since we find it mentioned in a charter of 1095, was owned from at least the year 1400 by the Châteaugiron, Frotier, and Malestroit families. On May 21, 1448, Jehan de Malestroit and his father Geoffrey sold it, not to Charles VII, as has been stated, but to Nicole Chambes, a gentleman of Scotch origin, and he, on October 19, 1450, resold it to André de Villequier. It was at this latter date that the Château of La Guerche was built and that Antoinette de Maignelais enters, or perhaps I ought to say re-enters on the scene. Agnes Sorel—poisoned, it is alleged, by Louis XI— had died in the previous February, murmuring to those around her the touching words " que c'était peu de chose, et orde et vile, que notre fragilité," and the fickle Charles had consoled himself by returning to his earlier sweetheart. Antoinette de Maignelais, who was Agnes Sorel's cousin, had presented her at Court and had been promptly supplanted in the King's affections. But the forsaken lady, " adroit and insinuating courtesan " as she was, knew how to bide her time, and a few months after Agnes' death had once more

gained her old power over Charles. The
Château of La Guerche was an earnest of his
future fidelity. The fact that the nominal
owner was André de Villequier does not
conflict with the assertion that it was built
for Antoinette, for this nobleman, whom you
can regard as either very unscrupulous or
very devoted to his sovereign, was her
husband. Their marriage took place about
the very time that the building of the château
was commenced, and it is a significant thing
that, " in consideration of the union," Charles
presented Villequier with the islands of
Oléron, Marennes, and Arvert, in addition
to the Viscountcy of St. Sauveur and the
Barony of Neahou. Antoinette was not one
to object to so equivocal an arrangement.
You may judge of her character by the fact
that, a year after her husband's death, she
publicly became the mistress of Francis II,
Duke of Brittany.

"But if these statements are correct," ask
the Sorelites, "how do you account for the
presence at La Guerche of Agnes' tomb and
statue ?" "That is easily answered," reply
the supporters of Antoinette de Maignelais.
"It is not Agnes' tomb at all, but that of
Jacqueline de Miolans, the first wife of Jean

Baptiste de Villequier, and who died, if you wish to know the exact date, in the year 1518."

Nevertheless, is it not curious that at La Guerche there should be this tradition as to Agnes Sorel's ownership of the château, and that she and Charles, moreover, should be said to have founded a chapel, the ruins of which are in the forest, in memory of a young girl who, whilst bird's-nesting in company with her betrothed, a falconer, was killed by a wolf?

Surrounded, until the beginning of the seventeenth century, by walls and a moat, the Château of La Guerche was accounted one of the strongest castles in the southern portion of Touraine. However, at the close of the sixteenth century, when it was still owned by the Villequier family, it was attacked and taken by assault. Claude de Villequier and his son Georges had joined the League, with the result that the district of La Guerche and that of Upper Poitou was in a continual state of agitation. Having captured all the castles for miles around, including those of Le Grand Pressigny and Etableaux, they appear to have made themselves particularly objectionable to the inhabitants, who fre-

quently complained of the ill-treatment they
received at the hands of the bands of ruffianly
soldiers whom Claude de Villequier had taken
into his service. But at last these complaints
were heard, and Arnaud de St. Lary, Lord of
Salers and Governor of the Castle of Loches,
set out with Louis Chateigner, Baron of
Preuilly, and their men to chastise the
Viscount of La Guerche and his turbulent son.
A stubborn fight took place beneath the castle
walls ; an entrance was forced ; and the
defenders were put to flight. The Viscount
of La Guerche and other noblemen were
drowned in the Creuse when attempting to
escape in a boat which had been kept in
readiness, and a similar fate was reserved for
more than four hundred out of the six
hundred and fifty Leaguers who lost their
lives on that eventful day.

This is the most stirring event I have to
record in the story of La Guerche. Its
history subsequent to the defeat of the
Leaguers was as calm and uneventful as it
had been in the days when Charles and
Antoinette lived beneath its roof, as I am
convinced they must many times have
done whilst André de Villequier was visiting
his islands off the coast of the ancient province

of Aunis. And may it never, was our wish
as we set off to see the gorges of the Creuse,
know ought save peaceful events, since those
are what best accord with its atmosphere of
quiet romance.

CHAPTER X

AT LA CHAPELLE-BLANCHE AND LOCHES

WHILST on the way to Loches we were reminded of the well-known fact that Touraine was at one time covered by the sea, and that over more than thirty thousand acres of its area there is scattered an easily discernible proof. We had to pass through the district of the *falunières*, those strata which contain billions of fossil shells, and which, at but a few inches below the surface of the ground, extend, in parts, to a depth of fifteen to twenty yards; so we stopped the car at least twice in search of specimens, and were rewarded by finding nearly thirty different kinds. Had we been expert geologists, with plenty of time to devote to natural history, I dare say we should have found many more, for no fewer than three hundred species of marine shells have been identified in these *faluns*. Scientists naturally regard them with

THE CHÂTEAU DE GRILLEMONT

great interest. So also do the agriculturists of La Chapelle-Blanche, Ste. Maure, Manthelan, and other communes where they exist, since experience has proved that they form a very excellent natural manure.

Loches was as a loadstone constantly drawing us towards it. Yet we felt that neither the *faluns* nor the Château de Grillemont ought to be passed by without notice, especially as both were on the main road and could be included in the day's excursion without encroaching on the time necessary for seeing that ancient town.

Grillemont is a fifteenth century château near La Chapelle-Blanche, some seven miles from Ligueil; it is a plain but distinctly dignified building with three solid, lofty towers, only one of which retains its machicolations; and it is situated in the midst of a somewhat deserted country, whose unattractiveness, however, is relieved, in the immediate neighbourhood of the castle, by the presence of woods. As in the case of the house in the Rue Briçonnet, at Tours, local tradition attributes its construction to Tristan l'Hermite. But that is an error. It received its name from Raoul de Grillemont, who lived in 1086, and who was the first known owner of the estate,

15

and its builder was Bertrand de Lescouet, the
son of Roland de Lescouet, Master of the
Hounds to the King of France. It is supposed to have been built between 1465 and
1470. François Balthazar Dangé d'Orsay,
councillor and secretary to Louis xv, owned
it in 1739, and he it was who, at a cost of
£12,000, restored and modified it. He destroyed a keep in order to make the present
courtyard, and he changed almost the entire
interior of the château to the style of his
period, a style which is best exemplified by
the drawing-room with its carved woodwork
and by the staircase with its wrought-iron
balustrade. The present owner, Comte P.
Lecointre, undertook, with the aid of M.
Guérin, an architect of Tours, a second
restoration, but without interfering, happily,
with the architecture of this fine building.
Its sole interest, in the absence of an eventful
history, lies in its architecture.

I am afraid that our *chauffeur*, after
we had said good-bye to the Château de
Grillemont, wilfully infringed the regulations as to speed, for he took us from La
Chapelle-Blanche to Loches, a distance of
thirteen miles, in a little over fifteen minutes.
Conscience and a wholesome fear of accidents

THE DRAWING-ROOM AT GRILLEMONT

THE STAIRCASE AT GRILLEMONT

would as a rule have prompted us to repress
him ; but we were anxious to get to our
destination, and he had so accurately read
our thoughts that we allowed him for
once to have his own way. Loches had
been painted for us in the most glowing
colours. "The most fascinating old town
in central France ; the one which has
the most surprises in store for you ; the
one which makes the deepest impression,
and which, consequently, is remembered the
longest,"—had been some one's estimate ;
and, though a trifle suspicious, through
past disappointments, of other people's
descriptions, it had keenly excited our
curiosity.

On reaching the old town of the left
bank of the Indre, it was a most agreeable surprise to us to find that our informer
had erred on the side of moderation. I
have a difficulty, indeed, in praising Loches
too highly. There are certainly more
interesting things to be seen there than
in any other small town we visited in
Touraine. In its quaint, narrow, irregular
streets, winding up the hillside towards
the ruins of the castle which crown the
summit, ancient buildings are met with

every few yards; and all are so good that
one can hardly say which is the best. Half
a day was all we could devote to Loches,
so, in order to economise time, we saw
its attractions in the order in which we
found them, beginning with the Porte des
Cordeliers, a turreted and machicolated gateway of the fifteenth century at the end of
the Rue de la Filature, and ending up with
the Collegiate Church and the Château
Royal. Passing beneath this gateway—one
of the principal former defences of the
town—we quickly came to a tower, the
Tour St. Antoine, which strongly reminded
us of Tours, in as much as it is the only
remaining tower of a church which was
built, between 1519 and 1530, in imitation
of the Cathedral of St. Gatien, and also
because of a certain resemblance it has to
the solitary Tour de l'Horloge and the Tour
Charlemagne. The Renaissance is very well
represented in Loches. Not far from the
Tour St. Antoine are several sixteenth
century houses, particularly in the Grande
Rue, which leads direct to the two most
noteworthy, the Hôtel de Ville and the
Chancellerie. The former adjoins the Porte
Picoys, another of the gateways with which

THE TOWN HALL AT LOCHES

the triple fortifications of the town were provided by Charles VII, and it was built between 1535 and 1543, under the orders of André Sourdeau and Bernard Musnier, at a cost of about 3800 livres tournois. The latter, which is in the steep, narrow street leading to the castle, dates from 1551, during the reign of Henry II, and is ornamented with a good deal of fairly well-preserved sculpture and royal mottoes.

Another ancient gateway, at the top and to the left of the Rue du Château, leads into the Rue Foulques Nerra and thence to a shady avenue at the end of which is the entrance to the castle. A gigantic keep, surrounded by a complicated system of defensive works, whose history forms the greater part of that of Loches itself, towers above the trees of this miniature boulevard with the menacing air it has retained during more than eight hundred years. It was built in the twelfth century on the solid basis of one of the master-pieces of that redoubtable builder of donjons, Fulk the Black. Seemingly impregnable, it was taken time after time, though it by no means invariably fell into the hands of besiegers, not even into those of the

fifteenth century. John Lackland, taking a
mean advantage of his brother's captivity,
got possession of it, but had quickly to
give it up in 1194 when Richard Cœur de
Lion returned to France. In 1204, after a
siege which lasted a year, it was captured by
Philip Augustus from Robert de Turneham
and Girard d'Athée, and was given, with
the town, to Dreux de Mello, in recognition of services rendered to the State by
his father, the former Constable of France.
St. Louis, however, purchased it for an
annuity of 600 livres forty-five years later,
and henceforth Loches and its castle were
crown property.

But for all that it continued to be the
scene of much strife. The English, who had
taken the Abbey of Beaulieu, on the opposite
bank of the Indre, made a vain attempt to
enter the town in 1412. Burgundians and
Armagnacs, in 1420, quarrelled as to who
should own the château, and as a result
burnt down the town. Charles VII rebuilt
it, and at the same time surrounded it
with walls and fortified gateways. His successor, Louis XI, devoted his attention to
strengthening the castle, not with the view
of preventing his enemies from breaking

into it—a step which the boldest would
have shrunk from taking—but in order to
prevent them getting out of it, once he
had placed them there. The Tour Ronde,
a large cylindrical tower to the right of
the keep, was built to his orders, its upper
rooms being placed at the disposal of
favoured prisoners, whilst the lowest cell
of all—a circular dungeon with a vaulted
roof hidden away in the foundations and
lit by the most depressing *meurtrières* I have
ever seen—was given to those who had
particularly incurred the sovereign's displeasure. From the roof of this under-
ground prison was suspended one of the
cages which Louis had amused himself by
inventing, and the manufacture of which he
watched with grim pleasure in the three
forges he had had established at the castle in
1479. These cages, which were sometimes
made of iron and sometimes of wood covered
with sheets of iron both inside and out,
were seven to eight feet long and about
the same in height, though some are said
to have been much smaller,—too small,
indeed, to allow the occupant either to
stand up or to lie down. Historians have
found references to at least nine distinct

cages de fer, but probably a very much
larger number existed at one time. That
used at Loches was for many years occupied
by Cardinal La Balue, after he had first
been imprisoned at Plessis-les-Tours, in consequence of his having sold Louis' secrets
to the Duke of Burgundy. It was destroyed
in 1790.

The cells of the Tour Ronde are, however,
the least impressive of the terrible prisons
of the Castle of Loches. The real *cachots*
are under the foundations of a fifteenth century
building called the Martelet, now in ruins,
and they consist of cell below cell, cut out
of the solid rock : the upper ones faced with
masonry fourteen feet thick and provided
with loopholes ; the lower ones almost as
dark and certainly as silent as a tomb. In
one of the latter, reached by descending a
narrow winding staircase with thirty-seven
steps, there was imprisoned for nine years
the one time Duke of Milan, Ludovic Sforza,
whom La Trémouïlle had taken prisoner in
the name of Louis XII. How monotonous
those years must have been is clear from
the rude paintings, designs, and inscriptions
with which the wretched man covered the
walls and part of the ceiling. On the wall

opposite the one narrow loophole that provides the cell with air is engraved a rude sundial, by means of which he hoped to keep track of time ; here and there is his portrait, or the Cordelier which those of his house adopted from St. Francis of Assisi ; and on all sides are lines and verses depicting, with poignant accuracy, his varying states of mind as the years rolled on. "Celui qui ne craint fortune," he has painted, in large letters, when in a philosophic mood, "n'est pas bien saige." In a similar spirit, he wrote the following :

"JE COGNAIS BIEN QUE PLVSIEVRS SONT DE CEVX EN CA
QUE TANT CVIDA
A QUI SOVBDAIN VNG BEAILLE CONGE
QUE VEVLT TVER SON CHIEN ON LVI MET SVS
N . SAV . SAN . N .
DE ESTRE ENRAGE
AINSI ESTRE DE LA POVRE PERSONNE
QUE ON VEVT HAÏR . SEE . XCV ."

"I know well that there are many, and it is a sharp grief,
To whom one gives their dismissal.
Who wishes to kill his dog first imputes to him the
charge of being mad,
So it is with the poor man
That one wishes to hate."[1]

---

[1] I am indebted for the following translations of the inscriptions and verses at Loches to Mrs. Watts-Jones' article, entitled "Thoughts in Prison," in the *English Illustrated Magazine* for 1891.

His verse shows more impatience, and there is sometimes a reproachful ring in it which makes one wish that Louis, whose claim to the throne of Milan was, as a matter of fact, invalid, had displayed a little more generosity towards him :

" JE . MEN . REPENS . CELA . NE . VAVLT . RIEN .
CAR . IAI . VOVLV . IONDRE . MON CVEVR . AV . TIEN .
POVR . MON . PLAISIR ET . TV . LVI . FAICTZ LA . GVERRE
SI . NE . TE . DOIS . DESORMAIS . PLVS . REQVERRE .
QVANT . VOVLENTE . ME . FAIRE . AVLCVN . BIEN .
TROP . DE PEINE . EVX . A . TROVVER . LE . MOIEN .
PARLER . A . TOI . CHERCHANT . TON . ENTRETIEN .
QUE . JAI . TROVVE . DIFICILE . A . CONQVERE ."

" I do repent, but what is that to thee?
My heart I would have joinèd unto thine,
But thou mad'st war upon this heart of mine.
Naught ask I henceforth, never seek thy face,
Since thou to me wouldst show no slightest grace ;
Yet for that bliss I strove with greater pain—
To see thee once—to speak with thee again—
Than o'er my foe to gain the victory."

Despair, too, is the note in the following touching lines :

" QUANT . MORT . ME . ASSAVLT . ET . QVE . IE . NE . PVIS .
MOVRIR.
ET . SECOVRIR . ON . NE . ME . VEVLT . MAIS . ME FAIRE .
RVDESSE .
ET . DE . LIESSE . ME . VOIR . BANNIR . QVE . DOIS . JE .
PLVS . QVERIR .
JA . NEST . BESOIN . MA DAME . REQVERIR . POVR . ME . GVERIR .
NE . POVRCHASSER . AVOIR . AVTRE ."

LOCHES

"When death assails me and I cannot die,
And none brings help, but rudeness and disdain,
And joy is banished, then what hope have I?
My lady cannot come to cure my pain
Nor can I seek another."

After nine years' captivity he was given
more cheerful quarters in an upper room
of the Martelet tower, and there, in 1510,
in the tenth year of his imprisonment, he
died of joy on hearing that at last he was
to be released.

Ludovic Sforza's reflections and lamentations are by no means the only ones you
can read in the prisons of Loches. There
is perhaps not a single one of their walls
that does not reverberate a note either of
anger, or sorrow, or despair. The earliest
inscription is dated 1417 and is in parts
undecipherable ; the latest was scratched by
a revolutionary in 1785 and prophesies the
early destruction of the castle walls, the
breaking of prison chains, and the abolition
of " ces tortures inventées par les Rois—trop
faibles pour arrêter un peuple qui veut sa
liberté." The prophecy was partly fulfilled,
but before it was how many had been forced
to respond to that ironical invitation written
on the wall of a passage leading to the

Tour Ronde : " Entrés, messieurs, chez le
roy nostre mestre " ! Even Philippe de
Commynes, who, during the minority of
Charles VIII, had offended the Lady of Beaujeu, was one of those who suffered imprisonment in the castle. He is supposed to be
the author of the words " Dixisse me aliqvando
penitvit tacvisse nvnqvam,"—" I have sometimes repented for having spoken, never for
having kept silent,"—which are beautifully
engraved in one of the cells. In another
prison is a Dutch inscription of the fifteenth
century declaring that

> " Money, malice, might,
>   Overcome law and right " ;

and in the same *cachot* is the following verse
in Catalanian, written by a prisoner of the
same period :

> " He who sighs hath never known . . .
>   Come within these walls of stone !
>   Here not only shall he sigh,
>   He shall groan in misery.
>   Sweeter far were it to die
>   Than in torment thus to lie.
>   Drear is death, yet far more drear,
>   Day by day to languish here.
>
>   .   .   .   .   .   .
>
>   The best of remedy in all our ill,
>   Is, seek the good within that none may kill."

After leaving the castle we visited part of its moat, which has been transformed into a profitable market-garden by Monsieur L. César. Gardener and explorer are the titles to which this amiable Lochois lays claim, for he takes a pride alike in the growing of fruit and vegetables and in the discovery of subterranean passages. On January 1, 1892, a turn of his spade brought to light the opening of a secret gallery which was built in the eleventh century for the purpose of revictualling the keep, and he has since opened it up to a length of more than two hundred yards. Archæology and gardening, he says, go admirably together. " I never know, in digging for potatoes, what treasure I may come across, what valuable addition I may make to my already well-stocked museum of curiosities."

The Collegiate Church of St. Ours can be seen whilst on your way to the Château Royal. To students of architecture it is an exceedingly interesting little building, since it is a composition of various styles dating from the tenth to the seventeenth centuries. In the porch there is even a specimen of Roman work : a cylindrical altar, made of a single block of stone,

ornamented with rudely carved figures of
warriors, and now used as a holy-water
stoup.

With this church is associated the name
of Agnes Sorel. For many years she lived
at Beaulieu, and at her death in 1450 she
expressed a wish to be buried in the
Collegiate. Her tomb, made of black marble,
on which is a most charming statue of
herself in white marble, representing her with
folded hands and with a little kneeling angel
on either side of her head, was, accordingly,
placed in the choir. But in 1777 the
Chapter, shocked at the idea of her ashes
being in that place, had them removed with
the tomb to the nave, and thence, a little
later, to one of the towers of the Château
Royal, where you can still see this beautiful
work of art. Approaching but not quite
equalling it in beauty is the Oratory of Anne
of Brittany, characteristically ornamented with
ermines and *cordelières*. These and the
enormous chestnut tree, which is said to
have been planted by Francis I, are the
most noteworthy things at the Logis du Roi,
as the château is sometimes called. As to
the building itself, which was inhabited by
Charles VII, Louis XI, Charles VIII, and

Louis xii, all of whom had a hand in its construction, it did not greatly impress us when viewed from the grounds, now those of the sub-prefecture of the Indre-et-Loire. To see it to the best advantage you must stand on the Grand Mail, where you get a true idea of its position on the hillside, at whose base lie the quaint gray houses of Loches and the many branches of the sluggish Indre.

CHAPTER XI

MONTRÉSOR AND ITS TREASURE

AN irregular line of white houses, surrounded by gardens and orchards, lies on the side of a sunlit hill ; a graceful château stands on the summit, protected by the ivy-covered walls and towers of a castle of feudal times ; and an irreproachably limpid little river, gemmed with white and yellow water-lilies, slowly meanders through a vine-clad valley. Such are the essential features of Montrésor, which is on the right bank of the Indrois, a tributary of the Indre, some fourteen miles to the west of Loches ; and on a sunny summer morning, especially when the orchards are white with blossom, or when the fruit is reddening on the tree, they form an unforgettable landscape.

Montrésor ! Did village ever receive a prettier name ? How it awakens your expectation on hearing it for the first time,

and how delightful a picture it calls up in
the minds of those who have been there
whenever it is repeated in after years ! Place
names are not, as a rule, the safest of guides
to the natural characteristics of localities ;
but in the case of Montrésor the appellation
is singularly appropriate. Philologically it
has, of course, nothing to do with either
natural beauties or a buried treasure, though
legend, which tells a pretty tale about King
Gontran falling asleep on the banks of a
stream, with his head on the knees of his
shield - bearer, and dreaming of a grotto
containing untold wealth, which he secured
through the assistance of a miraculous lizard,
puts in a claim for the latter derivation. It
is derived, say some philologists, from the
words " Mons Thesauri," its name from the
ninth to the eleventh centuries, and it was
so called because it was then the property
of the Treasury of the Cathedral of Tours.
" Unless," say others, " it comes from Mont
tréhort, tressort, or trésort,—that is to say,
the hill with three *cort*, or *hort*, which means
enceinte. In our opinion, the reference to
the triple fortifications which crown the
hill is palpable." The former explanation is
most probably the correct one, but since it
16

is always possible to point triumphantly to
the fortified hill, I suppose there will never
be wanting some one to take the opposite
view. The fortifications of the Château of
Montrésor are a very substantial reality, and
form an excellent basis for a weak argument.
You see the first of them on following the
winding village street and on coming face
to face with the stout outer wall of the old
castle. The second is not apparent until
you have passed through the modern entrance,
made in what was once part of the castle
itself, and are within the grounds. The
third is the later château, which, in spite
of its machicolated towers and its thick walls,
was built, however, more with the idea of
it serving as a residence than as a place to
resist an enemy's attacks.

It is difficult to say who laid the foundations of the older castle. There was a Lord
of Montrésor as early as 887, and he had
a stronghold somewhere on the hill above
the valley of the Indrois, but whether it
had any connection with that which is still
partly standing is not made clear by history.
Even his name has not been handed down.
Perhaps Roger, surnamed the Petit Diable,
who was a strong supporter of Fulk the

VIEW OF THE CHÂTEAU OF MONTRÉSOR ACROSS THE INDROIS

AN ANCIENT DOORWAY IN THE INNER
FORTIFICATIONS OF MONTRÉSOR

MONTRÉSOR: ENTRANCE TO THE CHÂTEAU

Black, had a hand in its construction. At
any rate he was one of its early owners.
After his day and that of his sons, it was
owned by Henry II of England, from whom
it was taken, however, in 1188, by Philip
Augustus. It next passed to members of
the Chauvigny and Palluau families. In
1190, a Chauvigny, André by name, accompanied Richard Cœur de Lion to the
Holy Land and fought there with great
bravery. At the end of the fourteenth
century, the castle belonged to the Beuil
family, and one of its members, Jean IV de
Beuil, made considerable improvements to
the outer wall, the way of the rounds, and
the towers. To make the place impregnable,
rather than agreeable as a residence, was the
ideal of the men of those days.

But the time was drawing near, after the
ownership of André de Villequier and his
sons, the Lords of La Guerche, and others,
when a change was to take place. Towards
the end of the fifteenth century, Imbert de
Batarnay, the nobleman who then owned it,
became dissatisfied with his prison-like castle,
and, having had many opportunities, whilst
sharing with Jean Bourré and Philippe de
Commynes the lifelong confidence of Louis XI,

of educating his taste for such things as
fine houses, decided to build a new one.   The
present château is a portion—unfortunately
only a portion—of this fifteenth century
building.   It originally extended along the
entire length of the plateau and it took thirty
years to complete.   The mutilations which it
has undergone were not wholly the work of
men of ignorant ages.   After passing through
the hands of various members of the Batarnay,
Bourdeilles, and Beauvillier families, the
château was sold, in 1831, to Count Jouffroy-
Gonssans, who was responsible for the destruction not only of one of the wings but of a
chapel which faced the courtyard to the west
of the existing building.   That they were in
a ruined state is possible, but it is a 'pity they
were not left standing for a few years longer,
for they might have been partly, if not wholly
restored at the time that Count Xavier
Branicki, who became the owner in 1849,
undertook the general restoration of the
château.   To this wealthy Polish gentleman
and his nephew, the present Count and owner
of Montrésor, is due the credit of having put
this historic house into the fine condition in
which we find it to-day.

Count Xavier Branicki, aided by the judg-

ment of his wife, did more, however, than
repair the château's crumbling architecture.
He turned it into a veritable treasure-house of
art, and, what is unique among the châteaux
of France, French and Italian art devoted to
Polish subjects.   It was a strange experience,
after steeping ourselves in the atmosphere of
the Middle Ages and the Renaissance whilst
viewing the château from various parts of the
grounds, to step into that of the tragic and
glorious history of Poland.   Nowhere, when
once the threshold has been crossed, can you
direct your eyes without encountering some
object which recalls either the sad or heroic
days of that oppressed country.   Side by side
with Paul Veronese's " Adulterous Wife " is
Tony Robert Fleury's " Massacre of the Poles
at Warsaw," and on the opposite wall of the
same room is a picture representing a cardinal
begging Sobieski, the King of Poland, to
relieve the city of Vienna.   John III is the
subject of the majority of the finest of the
works of art to be seen at Montrésor.

In the drawing-room, above a sixteenth
century Italian cabinet, are four magnificently
carved oak panels inspired by one of the
leading events in the life of that valiant Polish
sovereign.   The first of these bas - reliefs,

which are from one to two yards in length
and about a yard in height, depicts the victory
gained by Sobieski over the Turks on
September 12, 1683, whereby Europe was
saved from the Mohammedans.   The rival
armies are engaged in a hand to hand struggle
around the principal figures of the composition : John III and the Grand Vizir Kara-
Mustapha, whose head is about to be cleft in
twain by his royal adversary's upraised sabre.
Sobieski's triumphal entry into Vienna is the
subject of the second panel.   Wearing his
crown and royal mantle, the King advances
towards the city across the battlefield strewn
with dead and wounded.   He is accompanied
by his chief supporters, amongst others Prince
Maximilian of Bavaria, Prince George of
Saxony, and Prince Louis of Baden.   The
third bas-relief shows the victor's apotheosis.
Sobieski, who is dressed like a Roman
emperor, is being crowned by two women,
one of whom holds a palm, the other a
branch of laurel.   The throne on which he
stands upright, with his left hand resting on
a shield bearing his national arms, is supported
by five Turkish prisoners, who are attempting
to break their chains ; and the background,
against which his imposing figure stands out,

MONTRÉSOR: THE DRAWING-ROOM

A SIXTEENTH CENTURY ITALIAN CABINET AT THE CHÂTEAU OF
MONTRÉSOR

THE DINING-ROOM

consists of St. Peter's, representing Christian
Rome, and the statues of Bacchus and Pluto,
symbolising ancient Rome,—the two cities
in one which he saved from the infidel. As
spectators, and as it were sanctioning his
coronation, are two figures, representing
Heaven and Earth, one on either side of the
throne, and, near them, a Roman soldier, who
is wrapt in admiration. The fourth panel
completes the series in a very appropriate
manner by showing within medallions, supported by allegorical figures, the portraits of
John III and a young man with long flowing
hair, holding in his hand a commander's staff.
The latter is thought by some to be that
Prince Eugene who fought under Sobieski at
Vienna, and who became a field-marshal in
1687 at the early age of twenty-four. These
beautiful works were produced by Pierre
Vaneau, a native of Montpellier, where he was
born on December 31, 1653. He was a
protégé of Mgr. de Béthune, Bishop of Le Puy,
and was also commissioned to do many carvings (most if not all of them dealing with the
exploits of Sobieski) for the princes of Poland.
The Branicki family possess other works of
his at their Château of Villanof, near Warsaw.
Priceless as these four panels are, they

do not constitute, however, *the* treasure of
Montrésor. This is kept in a room adjoining the drawing-room, to the right of the
fireplace, on either side of which, by the
bye, we noticed family portraits by Ary
Scheffer. The entrance is hidden and cannot
be discovered, even though the woodwork
of the corner be examined ever so carefully.
Only those who are in the secret know
which part of the wainscot can be slipped
aside and the keyhole disclosed to view.
Then, when the key is inserted and turned
in the lock, a portion of the panelling
gives way, swings silently and heavily on
its hinges, like the door of a safe, and
allows you to pass through a many-feet-
thick wall into a chamber which will hold
at the most but half a dozen people. It
is lit by a small and jealously guarded
window, and against its walls stand the
glasscases which contain the solid gold
plate of the kings of Poland. Solomon's
golden vessels and those of the house of
the forest of Lebanon made, surely, no finer
show than these plates and vases and
goblets ornamented with exquisite designs,
and bearing, generally in company with
the crown and eagle of Poland, the names

of the sovereigns to whom they belonged.
There is a salt-cellar incrusted with medals
which stood on the table of Sigismund the
Great at the beginning of the sixteenth
century, and which, owing to the beauty
of its workmanship, is attributed to Benvenuto
Cellini. A plateau, decorated with sixteen
medals, bearing the effigy of Sigismund II,
dates from 1564 ; a larger one, resembling
it in shape and ornamentation, from 1628,
in which year it was made for Sigismund III,
as can be seen from his portrait and mono-
gram, an interlaced S and T (*Sigismundus
Tertius*), on each medallion. The cylindrical
vases are Nuremberg work of the seventeenth century. On the seventeen medals
with which two of these are enriched
are the profiles of Sigismund III, his son
Ladislas IV, who came to the throne in
1632, Duke George of Saxony, Queen
Christina of Sweden, and Frederic John
Langerhans, a German nobleman. Similarly,
a beer mug of pure gold recalls Ladislas IV,
Ferdinand I and Ferdinand II, the emperors
of Germany, and the first Centenary of the
Reform. The spoons, forks, and knives,
all made of the same precious metal, with
the exception of the blades of the last

named, also bear witness to their original
owner's desire for the richest work that
the goldsmith could produce. But what
is the glory of all these objects compared
with that of the principal piece of the
collection — Sobieski's soup-tureen? Here,
indeed, is a piece of plate worthy of being
set before a king! Its huge size, its beauty
of workmanship, and its historical value
combine to make it a work of unique
interest. It was the gift which the city
of Vienna made to John III in 1683 in
recognition of his victory over the Turks.
Four bas-reliefs depict the part played by
the great soldier in that momentous struggle.
One represents the meeting of the Polish
chiefs when they decided to go to the aid of
Austria; another, Sobieski's arrival; the third,
the fight under the walls of the capital;
and the fourth, the interview between the
King of Poland and the Emperor Leopold
after the battle. With great appropriateness, the legs supporting the tureen bear
the arms of the leading chiefs of the Polish
army. The cover is surmounted by a
statuette of Sobieski, in addition to being
ornamented with his portrait and that of
Leopold I.

That a treasure of this importance (its artistic and historical value is any sum you like to name provided it is not lower than £400,000, whilst its intrinsic worth is perhaps about half that amount)—that a treasure of this importance, I repeat, should have aroused a feeling of covetousness in the heart of a dishonest visitor to the Château of Montrésor is not at all surprising. Twenty years ago a daring attempt was made to steal it. The village locksmith, into whose jovial company we had the good luck to fall after leaving the castle, gave us a full account of the robbery; and that he was well qualified to do so is evident from the part he played soon after its discovery, for he it was who was called in to provide the treasure-room with its present ingeniously concealed and armour-plated door, and that complicated system of electric burglar alarms which are believed to be proof against the smartest cracksman who ever used a jemmy. The precautions taken twenty years ago to guard the treasure were, he said, practically nil. The guardian whose duty it was to look after it at night-time was notoriously fond of the bottle, and the nearer midnight

approached the less capable he was, as a
rule, of answering for his faculties. The
treasure-room door presented not the slightest
difficulty to the veriest tyro in burglary.
And as to electric or other alarms to doors
and windows, they were, of course, unheard
of in that part of the country in those
days. This state of unpreparedness naturally
attracted the attention of those who are
ever on the look - out for easy cribs to
crack. One summer day a stranger arrived
in the village and took up his residence
at one of the inns, where he announced
his intention of stopping for a few days
" to study the antiquities of the district."
Archæology was his passion. He made
long excursions in the neighbourhood in
search of ancient buildings, such as the
ruins of the Château of Villiers, to the
south of the village ; he meditated over
the beauties of the Collegiate Church of
Montrésor ; and he went into ecstasies
over the château and the castle, whose
walls — and especially those on the side
where the treasure-room is situated — he
was noticed to examine with all the love
of a born antiquarian. The treasure itself,
too, interested him not a little, as was

observed on the one public occasion on
which he was remembered to have visited
it. Early one morning, some three or four
days after his arrival, the big bell of the
château sounded the alarm. Taking advantage of the more than usually copious
libations in which the guardian had in-
dulged over night, some one who had
evidently concealed himself in the château
when it was closed for the day, the owners
being then absent, had broken into the
room containing the treasure and had made
his escape through the narrow window
with several of the most precious pieces
of the collection. In case he was disturbed
during his operations, he had prepared to
sell his life dearly. Nearly all the weapons
above the mantelpiece and on the walls had
been removed and distributed in various
parts of the drawing-room, so that wherever
he might be, if surprised and driven into
a corner, a dagger or a sabre would be
within reach of his arm. Suspicion, in
the mind of the now thoroughly sobered
guardian, fell upon the stranger of antiquarian
tastes, and, as he was missing from his inn,
a hue and cry was set up after him. He
had several hours' start. Had he lived in

the days of motor-cars that would have been
ample to have enabled him to get away not
only with what he had in his possession,
but with the entire gold plate of the kings
of Poland. But he had only his legs to
carry him to Loches, so had to face the
inevitable. Two detectives met him on the
bridge in that ancient town and taxed him
with the robbery. He blandly protested.
Protest was, however, useless. They opened
his coat—suspiciously bulky—and there, one
under each arm, were the golden plateaus
of the two Sigismunds. He was sentenced,
some months later, to twenty years' penal
servitude.

Before leaving Montrésor to return to
Loches and continue our travels along the
valley of the Indre we visited the beautiful
Collegiate Church which was founded by
Imbert de Batarnay early in the sixteenth
century. Its exterior is particularly remarkable for a fine entrance with bas-
reliefs representing scenes in the life of
Christ; its interior, for the still more
charming tomb of the Batarnays, a rec-
tangular tomb ornamented with statuettes
of the apostles in niches, and bearing the
couchant statues of Imbert de Batarnay,

Georgette de Montchenu, his wife, and François, their son. Some historians have said that the third statue is that of Claude de Batarnay, who, wounded at the battle of St. Denis, died in Paris on November 18, 1567, in his twenty-second year. But that is an error. There is no document to prove that other remains than his heart were brought back to Montrésor, and this, as we know, was placed in a marble urn in the church of his ancestors. It is now in a little oratory at the top of one of the towers of the château. For our special benefit the heavy lid of this urn was removed, the box inside was taken out, and the heart of the young captain was placed in our hands. It was a rare sensation,—one we would not willingly have missed. To think that that misshapen ruddy mass, dried and hardened by more than three hundred years of repose in its faintly fragrant sepulchre, had once throbbed with the quick-flowing blood of a young man !

CHAPTER XII

IN THE VALLEY OF THE INDRE: FROM MONTBAZON TO RIGNY-USSÉ

BALZAC'S well-known description, in *Le Lys dans la Vallée*, of the valley of the Indre has the defect which one would expect to find in the work of a native of Touraine,—a defect, moreover, which is inherent in most romances of that kind : it is a little too rose-coloured to be a true picture of Nature.

This valley, "which begins at Montbazon, and ends at the Loire, is," he says through the mouthpiece of Félix de Vandeness, "a magnificent emerald cup, with the Indre, winding like a serpent, at the bottom. . . . To me, infinite love . . . is expressed by this long ribbon of water, sparkling in the sunlight between two green banks, by these

rows of poplars which adorn this valley of
love with their mobile lacework of leaves,
by the oak woods which jut out into the
vineyards on hillsides round which the river
winds ever differently, and by the shaded
horizons which fade into the distance. If
you would see Nature as beautiful and
as virginal as a bride, visit this valley on
a spring day ; if you would soothe the
wounds of your heart, return there during
the last days of autumn. . . . At that
moment," — the moment when the hero
was gazing on the beauties of his favourite
landscape,—" the mills of the falls of the
Indre lent a voice to this valley quivering
with life, the poplars swayed laughingly, the
birds warbled, and the cicidas sang. Everything was melodious. And not a cloud
obscured the sky. . . . Deeply moved, I
descended to the bottom of this basket of
flowers, and soon saw a village which,
overflowing with poetry as I was, I found
without an equal. Imagine three mills set
in the midst of graceful, wooded islands,—
masses of greenery on a field of water.
What other name can I give to that expanse
of aquatic vegetation, so vivacious and so
finely coloured, which carpets the river,

17

undulates with it, lends itself to its caprices, and bends before the tempests raised by the mill-wheels? Here and there are masses of gravel against which the water breaks, forming fringes in which the sun sparkles. Daffodils, white and yellow water-lilies, rushes and phlox decorate the banks with their magnificent carpets. A decayed and trembling bridge, with flower-covered piers, and hand-rails which, overgrown with weeds and velvety mosses, lean over the river and yet do not fall; worn out boats and fishermen's nets; the monotonous song of a shepherd; the ducks which swim about among the islands, or preen their feathers on the *jard*, the name given to the rough sand drifted by the Loire; and miller-boys, with their caps stuck on the sides of their heads, loading their mules: each of these details made the scene surprising in its naïveté. Imagine, beyond the bridge, two or three farms, a dovecote, some turtle-doves, and thirty tumble-down cottages, separated by gardens and by hedges of honeysuckle, jessamine, and clematis; imagine a flowered manure-heap before every door, and cocks and hens in every road,—and you have the village of Pont de Ruan before you. . . .

THE RUINS OF MONTBAZON

Frame the whole with ancient walnut trees and young poplars with pale golden leaves, place a few graceful manufactories in the midst of those extensive fields which fade into the distance under a hot and vaporous sky,—and you will be able to form an idea of one of the thousand points of view in this beautiful district."

Unless the valley of the Indre has lost a good deal of its picturesqueness since Balzac's day, and I doubt if it has much changed during the last sixty to seventy years, his estimate of its beauty is certainly exaggerated. Following it from Montbazon to Rigny-Ussé, we had countless opportunities of noting its characteristics, which are those of any pleasant little valley, watered by a pretty meandering stream. Do not be led, therefore, through the idealism of the author of *Le Lys dans la Vallée* to expect too much ; and remember that he was a Tourangeau.

Montbazon is interesting principally on account of its ruined, ivy-covered castle, whose square keep, which was built by Fulk the Black in 988, is one of the most curious of the military buildings of the tenth century in this part of France. It

stands on a hill overlooking the village
and the valley, and is an essentially
picturesque feature of the landscape as,
travelling along the road from Cormery,
it gradually comes into view. But it would
be even more picturesque without the in-
congruous bronze statue of the Virgin which
some devout Catholic has had placed on
the highest point of the keep. Intended
to be a perpetual inspirer of pious thoughts,
I am afraid that in our case it failed in its
object; for our minds were wholly occupied
with the exploits of the builder of the
fortress and with the romantic story of the
beautiful Duchess of Montbazon, Marie de
Bretagne, the second wife of Hercule de
Rohan. With Fulk you are already sufficiently well acquainted, but I dare say
that the name of the lady is heard by you
for the first time. She was celebrated for
two things: her utter disregard of morality,
and her ideal beauty. The former caused
Cardinal de Retz to say of her: "I have
never met a person who showed in the
practice of vice so little respect for virtue;"
the latter turned the heads of innumerable
lovers. One of her greatest admirers, and
the one with whom her name is usually

connected, was the Abbé de Rancé, who
was fifteen years younger than herself, and
whom she had brought up with her own
children from the age of nine. His sorrow
at her death from fever on April 28, 1656,
was so great that he withdrew to a Trappist
monastery for the remainder of his life.
The scene of their amour was the Château
de Couzières, which stands a little more
than a mile to the north-east of Montbazon,
on the right bank of the Indre. A visit
there is not absolutely essential, but when
you are so near it is just as well perhaps
to include Couzières in your programme.
It was partly built during the first half of
the seventeenth century on the foundations
of an older château, and, as an inscription
on a marble tablet informed us, it has an
historical as well as a romantic interest,
since it was there, on September 5, 1619,
that the interview between Louis XIII and
Marie de' Medici took place, an interview
which resulted in the confirmation of the
treaty of Angoulême and the momentary
reconciliation of mother and son.

Both Montbazon and Couzières are, however, but an introduction to the castles and
country-houses of the valley of the Indre.

More important châteaux, including two which
rank with the finest in Touraine, lie farther
down stream, and to these we hastened.   A
few miles' run brought us to Monts and
the first of this succession of noteworthy
residences : the Château de Candé, which,
standing on the top of a hill, in full view of
the valley and the imposing viaduct which
crosses it at this point, enjoys a position that
could not well be finer.   This beautiful house
was built by François Briçonnet early in the
sixteenth century.   He was Mayor of Tours
and came of a family of able men, one of them
a cardinal.   A second holder of that position,
Charles Mesnager, owned the château in 1542,
and from the hands of his daughter Catherine,
the widow of François Péguineau, it passed,
in 1556, to Guillaume Bertrand.   The new
owner kept it, however, only eight years, for
he resold it in 1564 to Victor Brodeau, whose
descendants were to retain it for one hundred
and fifty years.   The Brodeau family prided
itself on its descent from that Jean Brodeau
who fought and died at the siege of St. Jean
d'Acre, and its members on that account were
authorised by Philip Augustus to use as their
arms " a cross crosslet and three palms," which
you can see on the fireback in the drawing-

THE CHÂTEAU DE CANDE FROM THE PARK

THE CHÂTEAU DE CANDÉ FROM THE GARDEN

DRAWING-ROOM AT THE CHÂTEAU DE CANDÉ

room.   After May 16, 1715, when the
château passed out of the Brodeau family,
it became, successively, the property of
the Anguille de la Niverdière, Pouget de
Montsoudun, and Caron de Fleury families,
and was finally bought, in 1853, by the
present owner, M. Drake del Castillo.   This
gentleman undertook its restoration and has
improved it in a hundred ways.   In addition,
he has filled his house with valuable art
objects and pictures.   The admirable firedogs in the drawing-room are attributed to
Benvenuto Cellini.   Above the mantelpiece,
which is a finely carved copy of one at Bruges,
stands a unique bronze bust of Louis XII.
And the pictures in the same room include
works by Van der Velde and Léopold Robert.

At your next stopping-place, Azay-le-
Rideau, you would do well to linger, as we
did, for the greater part of a day.   An entire
afternoon is none too long to devote to this
superb château and its delightful surroundings :
a diamond in an emerald setting.

There is an account of how the Château
of Azay-le-Rideau came to be built in
Balzac's *Contes Drolatiques*, but it has nothing
whatever in common with a book of travel.
Mere historical accuracy is a feature of

secondary consideration in those joyous
Rabelaisian tales. Nevertheless, for the sake
of a few happy descriptive phrases, which
show how much the great writer loved the
building that he elsewhere calls a "diamant
taillé à facettes, serti par l'Indre, monté sur
des pilotis masqués de fleurs," some lines from
his amusing *nouvelle* "Comment feut basty le
Chasteau d'Azay" are worth quoting :—

"At that time"—that is, in the days of
Jacques de Beaune's supposed meeting with
the Lady of Beaujeu—he writes, "the Château
of Chenonceaux was being built by Messire
Bohier, the Minister of Finances, who, as
a novelty, pretentiously placed his house
astride the river Cher. Now, the Baron of
Semblançay, wishing to do the very opposite
of what the said Bohier had done, boasted of
having built *his* mansion on the bed of the
Indre, where—the gem of that beautiful green
valley—it still stands, so solidly was it constructed on piles. Consequently, Jacques de
Beaune, apart from the duty-service of his
retainers, spent upon it 30,000 crowns. And
thus, forsooth, is this château one of the most
graceful and most elaborated of the châteaux
of beautiful Touraine ; and thus does it ever
bathe in the Indre like a *galloise princière*,

adorned with lace-like pavilions and windows,
and with pretty soldiers on its weather-cocks,
that turn—like all soldiers—whichsoever way
the wind blows them."

This curious name of Azay-le-Rideau has
nothing to do with a curtain, but is derived
from Hugues Ridel, or Rideau, who was
created a knight-banneret in 1213, and who
built a castle there to defend the passage of
the Indre. The position was an important
one from a strategic point of view, and when
Jean-sans-Peur seized Tours in 1417 he took
care also to place a garrison of three hundred
and fifty-four men at Azay. The Burgundian
soldiers evidently had a higher opinion of
the strength of the fortress than it justified,
for they ventured to jeer from its walls at
the Dauphin Charles as he passed a year
later on his way from Chinon to Tours.
Greatly irritated by these insults, the prince
at once laid siege to the castle and captured
it, in spite of a desperate resistance on the
part of the defenders, who knew what they
had to expect. Every one of them was
hanged, their captain was beheaded, and
the castle was razed to the ground. Whether
a second castle was built seems doubtful.
This, however, is certain : the estate passed

through a number of hands in the course of
the next eighty years, and towards the end
of the fifteenth century it came into the
possession of Jean Berthelot, one of the
King's treasurers. His son, Gilles Berthelot,
was also a financier, and acquired an immense
fortune. Legend says that he was not very
particular as to the means by which he obtained his wealth, but much may be forgiven
him for the way he employed it, for we owe
to him the present château—a masterpiece
which is not excelled for grace, delicacy, and
harmony by any of the celebrated châteaux
of central France. One of the great charms
of its peculiar beauty is its exclusively national
character. At the time when it was built
French art was imbued with the principles
of the Renaissance, and was stirred to emulation of the masterpieces of Italy ; but that
emulation found expression, as we have
already seen in the case of Blois, Chambord,
and Amboise, in originality, not in an imitation of the work of Rome or Florence. As
the château was to be constructed for a man
of peace, the architect could give full scope
to his fancy, and was not under the necessity
of trying to combine the fortress with the
dwelling-house. He placed it on an island

A PICTURESQUE CORNER OF AZAY-LE-RIDEAU

on one of two little branches of the Indre, and this position adds greatly to its picturesqueness. Though ever a beautiful object, it perhaps looks its best in early autumn, when the mellow tints which four centuries have given to the stonework harmonise with the russet hues of the foliage. Lord Leighton once said that the surest proof of the beauty of a work of art was the emotion it created in the mind of the beholder. The test is a severe one, for much, of course, depends upon the æsthetic education of the spectator ; but I fancy there are very few people who would be able to restrain an involuntary start of admiration on first catching sight of Azay-le-Rideau across the sunlit, lilied waters of the Indre. There are few works of art in which it is impossible to pick holes, and some superfine critics have objected that Azay-le-Rideau has too much " top-hamper," and would be improved if the roofs, turrets, and machicolations were reduced. But the general opinion is that the building is an almost perfect specimen of Renaissance architecture, and that no alteration would be likely to improve it.

But if equal to any of the other châteaux of Touraine in architectural beauty, Azay-le-

Rideau is inferior to them in respect to historical associations. No tragedies have occurred within its walls ; no royal processions of note have marched across its bridge. Kings have, doubtless, crossed its threshold, but they came only to pay a visit of courtesy to the castellan ; and history has not recorded any great events in which Azay-le-Rideau played even an unimportant part. Nor does its private history present much interest, except the sad story of its founder. For Gilles Berthelot did not long enjoy the palace he had erected. His cousin, Jacques Semblançay, whom Balzac erroneously states was the builder of Azay, was accused, as treasurer to Francis 1, of malversation. The King ordered six commissioners to examine his accounts, and amongst them Gilles Berthelot. Whether he accepted the position with a view to screen or assist his relative, or whether the office was thrust upon him with a view to bring about his downfall, history does not say. It is not improbable that some courtier had coveted poor Berthelot's château, and had plotted to bring about the ruin of its master and the confiscation of his property. At any rate, that is exactly what happened. Semblançay

THE ENTRANCE TO AZAY-LE-RIDEAU

A RENAISSANCE CABINET AT AZAY-LE-RIDEAU.

A MANTELPIECE AT AZAY-LE-RIDEAU

was executed, his sons were banished, and, very soon afterwards, Berthelot himself received a hint that he, too, might swing on the gibbet at Montfaucon. He fled to Metz and so saved his life, but soon learned that his goods were confiscated and his château had been bestowed on Antoine Raffin, the captain of a hundred men of King Francis' guard. The loss of this beautiful dwelling was more than he could bear, and he is said to have died of a broken heart.

Antoine Raffin evinced his gratitude to his royal benefactor by placing a salamander over the door of the château and on various other parts of the building, both inside and out. Whether he long enjoyed the estate I know not, for no one, not even the erudite Abbé Chevalier, has had the time or the patience to search out the names of the many owners of the château during the last three centuries.

The more recent history of Azay-le-Rideau is better known. Some thirty to forty years ago its owner was the Marquis de Biencourt, and he it was who began its restoration. Time had dealt kindly with the château and added more beauty than it had destroyed. The carved doors at the entrance, as his

initial upon them shows, date from his
ownership ; so also do the restored medallions
of the kings and queens of France—defaced
during the Revolution — on the ceiling of
the staircase. These carvings were the work
of M. Bernard Depont, a sculptor of considerable talent, who carried out many
commissions for similar work in the châteaux
of Touraine, notably at Comacre and at
Réaux. He was a son of the official sculptor
at the Court of Saxe-Weimar, and on settling
down at Azay, about the middle of the last
century, quickly gained a widespread reputation for being a skilful worker in wood and
in stone. Some of his carvings went to
England, where, at the residence of Sir
Watkin Williams, they are doubtless still
to be seen.

In the Marquis de Biencourt's day, the
château was full of splendid furniture and
fine pictures. There came a time, however,
—it was on the occasion of the failure of
the Union Générale,—when these had to
be dispersed. One of the sideboards was
sold for more than £3000, and is now,
I am told, in the Louvre ; a bedstead dating
from the reign of Francis was presented to
the Cluny Museum.

Azay-le-Rideau then fell upon evil days.
It came into the hands of speculators.   One
of its temporary owners—or perhaps he was
merely the tenant—attempted to turn it
into a school for young English aristocrats ;
but the experiment ended in a wholly
unforeseen manner, after it had been open
only one summer.   On returning, one day,
from Tours, where they had been allowed
to spend an afternoon of perfect freedom,
the pupils were in such high spirits that
nothing would satisfy them but to cast
most of the furniture out of the windows !

Judging by the poor furniture and still
poorer pictures which we found in the
château, it had never been refurnished since
that day of destruction.   It had the air of
having been temporarily furnished in view
of the arrival of some prospective American
purchaser.   In fact, the official guide
remarked to us : " If only a wealthy American
would buy Azay, as Chenonceaux was bought
by M. Terry, then we should see it worthily
embellished."   That much-desired millionaire
did not put in an appearance, but a re-
presentative of the French Government did,
and thus Azay-le-Rideau, as a museum of
the Renaissance, under the authority of the

Minister of Fine Arts, will henceforth live
over again its palmiest days.

That the French Government—notoriously
short of money as it is—should have been
able to purchase the Château of Azay-le-
Rideau is surprising.   As will at once be
concluded, it was only owing to exceptional
circumstances that it was able to do so.
These are worth mentioning.

Two years ago a wealthy connoisseur,
named M. Dru, bequeathed his Château de
Vez, in the Oise, to the State, on condition
that it was classed among the historical
monuments of France.   He also directed
that a sum of 40,000 francs a year be paid
out of his fortune to the Government for the
restoration and upkeep of his property.

This princely legacy, strange to say,
somewhat embarrassed the Department of
Fine Arts ; for the Château de Vez, although
interesting, is not a building of great
architectural value, and was in no need of
so large a sum as 40,000 francs a year for its
maintenance.   What was to be done ?   The
question puzzled the authorities for many
months, but it was finally solved by M. Dru's
heirs making the following proposal, which,
needless to say, was immediately accepted :

instead of paying 40,000 francs a year to the State, they offered a lump sum of 1,000,000 francs, 100,000 francs of which was to be expended on the Château de Vez, henceforth to be inhabited by them and kept in thorough order.

It was with 200,000 francs of this 900,000 francs capital that the State purchased Azay-le-Rideau from a M. Artaud. The balance has been invested, so that there will be an income amply sufficient not only for the thorough restoration of the château, but also for its organisation as a museum of the Renaissance. Already much has been done towards those ends. The State architects have been busy for some time past in removing modern additions, and in the course of their work have made some interesting discoveries, including an ancient well and *lavabo* on the site of the former kitchens; while several of the rooms have been arranged with works of art from the Louvre and private collections. Among the donors of pictures, tapestries, carved furniture and other works of art are Baron Edmond de Rothschild, Baron Henri de Rothschild, Madame Ernesta Stein, M. Kleinberger, M. Jacques Seligmann, M. Wildenstein and M. Fernand Kalphen.

18

Whilst at Azay-le-Rideau a walk of less than a mile in the direction of the railway station will bring you to a small sixteenth century château called Islette. This large country-house with stout machicolated towers and high-pitched roofs is also situated on the Indre, and adjoining it is an ancient mill, which is alone worth seeing. Above a doorway, facing the lawn and gardens, is an excellent specimen of Renaissance sculpture. The most interesting work of art in the interior of the château, which the owner most obligingly allowed us to visit, though it is not usually open to the public, is an elaborately painted mantelpiece, the only one of its kind I have seen.

On reaching the terminus of our journey down the valley we met with one of the few *contretemps* of our three months' holiday in Touraine. The Château d'Ussé was closed on that particular day. It was lost labour to explain to the caretaker that we had been misled by the French guide-book which we had taken with us for the sake of its supposed practical information, and to point out that it was really a pity we should have come so far to see merely the outside of the castle. The sole person in

THE PAINTED MANTELPIECE AT THE CHÂTEAU
DE L'ISLETTE

RENAISSANCE SCULPTURE ABOVE A DOORWAY AT
ISLETTE

THE CHÂTEAU OF USSÉ

authority, in the absence of her master,
the Comte de Blacas, she was obdurate.
So we had to be content with a view
of the exterior of Ussé, a short walk in
its gardens, and a visit to its charming
chapel. Fortunately, this was sufficient to
satisfy our appetite for beautiful things,
and enabled us to forgo with a light
heart the splendidly decorated King's bedroom, certain superb mantelpieces, and a fine
staircase on which is a picture of St. John
attributed to Michael Angelo. The white
towers and gray slate roofs of graceful Ussé
rise from the greenery of their wooded hillside like those of a château in a fairy-tale.
The façades of the Cour d'Honneur, overgrown in parts with creepers, are also very
picturesque. This courtyard faces the fine
terraces which overlook the Indre, but a
few yards wide at this point of its course,
and which were built by Marshal de Vauban,
whose daughter, Jeanne Françoise, married
a member of the Bernin de Valentinay
family, to whom the château belonged at
the end of the seventeenth and the beginning
of the eighteenth centuries. These terraces
form but a very small part of the grounds
of Ussé, which are so extensive that the

walls enclosing them are nearly seven miles
in circumference. The chapel is a beautiful
Renaissance structure, eminently worthy of
careful study and, as regards style, comparison
with the château itself. Ussé was built by
Jacques d'Espinay, Chamberlain to Louis XI
and Charles VIII, at the end of the fifteenth
and the beginning of the sixteenth centuries,
and its architecture consequently follows the
traditions of the Gothic rather than those
of the Renaissance style. Only in details
of decoration does the spirit of the new
manner make its appearance. On the other
hand, in the case of the chapel, which
was built between 1520 and 1538, in accordance with the testamentary wishes of Jacques
d'Espinay, the Renaissance style is dominant.
It is not often that one can note so strikingly
as this the progress which has been made
in a branch of art during so short a period
as thirty years.

CHAPTER XIII

UP THE CHER: FROM VILLANDRY TO VÉRETZ

EVENING having closed in when we left the banks of the Indre and reached those of the Cher, the start on the last of our journeys along the rivers of Touraine was naturally postponed until the next morning. Before leaving Villandry, however, we paid a brief visit to its stately château, which dates in the main from the end of the sixteenth century. The oldest portion is a square tower of the fourteenth century, facing the park to the right of the entrance; the latest, the terraces, which were added about the middle of the eighteenth century, and from which, on a clear day, a good view can be obtained of the Loire and the châteaux of Luynes and Langeais. The best preserved part is the courtyard. But that is not saying much, for, truth to tell, Villandry is, or was at the time we saw it, in a deplorable state of preservation. The ancient family which formerly lived there had parted with the property, and the speculators into whose hands it had fallen had allowed it to deteriorate little by little. The grounds had been reduced in size, owing to successive sales, and what remained, some seventy acres and the château, was to be put up for auction on the very day after our visit. As in the case of Azay-le-Rideau, the *concierge* confessed that everybody hoped that a wealthy American would turn up at the opportune moment, " for only the Americans are sufficiently wealthy to restore these old châteaux and keep them up in the ancient style." The interior of the château has no special interest for the sightseer, but its gardens and grounds are delightful. The recollection of a certain avenue of lime trees, one hundred and fifty yards long, will linger in our memories for many and many a year.

Less than two miles along the road from Villandry to Savonnières we came to the famous *caves gouttières* of the last named place. They extend for more than a hundred yards into the hillside, and consist of a number of caverns, through the roofs of which the water, charged with carbonate

THE CHÂTEAU DE VILLANDRY FROM THE PARK

A CORNER OF THE GARDENS AT VILLANDRY

of lime, incessantly filters, forming on all
sides the most beautiful deposits of calcareous
spar.   Bernard Palissy visited them in 1547,
and, as he states in one of his works, was
delighted with these marvels of Nature.
The ancient village of Savonnières to which
you come about a third of a mile farther
on, is well worth making into a halting
place, in order to see the old mill-wheel
and the sculptured entrance to a twelfth
century church.   It was founded by the
Romans, who are said to have had a soap
manufactory there,—hence its name.

Leaving the Cher at Savonnières, the road
does not rejoin the river for a considerable
distance, not, in fact, until it reaches St.
Avertin, one of the prettiest of the suburbs
of Tours.   We took advantage of this deviation and went a little out of our way to see
the Château de la Carte, near Ballan.   This
pleasant little manor-house stands on historical
ground, and I counsel you to visit it as
much on that account as because of its own
particular interest.   Traces of a Roman road
which led from Tours to Poitiers have been
found near the château, which was probably intended to defend it, since it stands
at the culminating point of the extensive

plateau that separates the valleys of the
Loire and the Indre. It was this road which
was followed by the Saracens in the eighth
century, when they were defeated by Charles
Martel. The battle took place (October
10, 732) on the Landes de Charlemagne,
which are contiguous with the walls surrounding the grounds of the château. These
landes are now planted with vines and
corn ; and it was no unusual thing, some
years ago, for the labourers to unearth
feudal weapons and bones whilst they were
preparing the ground for their masters'
crops. Facing them, at the southern ex-
tremity of the château's walls, are two
ancient towers, provided with loopholes for
archers and called by the inhabitants of the
district " Charlemagne's Towers." Whether
these are as old as they are said to be I
have not succeeded in learning either from
M. Pierre Duché, the present owner of
Carte, or from historical records ; but I
doubt if they date so far back as the eighth
century. Other traces of feudal times were
once visible within the grounds, notably a
well, called " Le Puits des Sarrasins," which,
according to legend, was connected with or
was near to a subterranean passage that is

THE CHÂTEAU DE LA CARTE

THE CHÂTEAU DE LA CARTE: THE ENTRANCE

"CHARLEMAGNE'S TOWER" AT THE CHÂTEAU DE LA CARTE

said to have communicated with Tours.
This has long since disappeared and must
not be confounded with the picturesque
old pump and well which exist to the
right of the château.   But at the entrance
to the park there still remains another proof
of the antiquity of this country-house and
estate : two towers with heavy wooden door,
studded with nails and bound with iron,
and dating, it is said, from feudal days.
On either side I noticed traces of a moat,
which was evidently once crossed by a
drawbridge.   Passing between these towers
you see in front of you an extensive lawn
and the château, a rather small but homely
looking house, which was built, in part,
at the end of the fifteenth century.   The
oldest portion is the square tower, or keep,
surmounted by a belfry, at the back of
the building.   The bell in this belfry
weighs nearly half a ton and bears the
following inscription in Gothic characters :
"Ave Maria, cest bonne chanson, gratia
plena, Dominus tecum, MVCXVIII."   The
arms of Jacques de Beaune, the unfortunate
treasurer to Francis I, can still be distinguished
upon it, though they were much mutilated
at the time of the Revolution.   Authority

to build the château was granted to the
Baron of Semblançay by Françoise de la
Rochefoucauld, Lady of Montbazon, on
November 28, 1497. Eighteen months later,
Louis XII granted him other privileges, so
he set to work to build a château with
towers, keep, walls, park, dykes, and fortified
gates. The little chapel to the left of
the front door also dates from his time.
Jacques de Beaune did not, however, long
enjoy his new house, for his property was
confiscated. Nor did his son, Guillaume
de Beaune, to whom part of his father's
possessions, including the Château de la
Carte, was returned by Francis, have much
better fortune. He was similarly accused
of embezzling public money, but saved
his neck by fleeing, and was banished.
Again confiscated, Carte was this time sold,
and during the next three hundred years
was owned by many famous families. The
historian Georges Oudard Feudrix de Bre-
quigny, a member of the French Academy,
was the owner in 1760.

There is a tradition that Simon de Brion,
who became Pope in 1281 under the title
of Martin IV, was born in the château.
But this is not known for certain. If he

were, then he must have first seen the light in an earlier manor-house, which was owned by his father, N. de Brion, who is the first known possessor of this ancient estate.

The interior of the Château de la Carte has been completely modernised and therefore contains neither sculptured mantelpieces nor painted ceilings. In lieu of these, however, there are some very fine tapestries, two or three *bahuts* which came from the Château of Azay-le-Rideau, an arm-chair which was used by Balzac on the many occasions he visited at the château, and two interesting firebacks, including one bearing the arms of Gilles Boutaut, or Boutault, who was almoner to Louis XIII, Canon and Archdeacon of Tours, Abbé of St. Remy of Sens, Bishop of Aire in 1626, and Bishop of Evreux in 1649. This distinguished ecclesiastic, who was born at Tours, or in the suburbs, in 1594, died in Paris on March 11, 1661. The chapel contained, during the ownership of the Comtesse de Picquetières, two beautiful stained-glass windows, representing the Nativity and the Adoration, but these were sold some fifteen to twenty years ago before M. Duché bought the property. On the other hand, this gentleman prevented the dispersion of another equally precious work of art by purchasing, after the Countess' death, a terra-cotta Virgin of the fifteenth or sixteenth century. This charming statuette he has left in its most fitting place, the chapel, whilst a copy of it he has had placed over the doorway. In the chapel is also an ancient fresco which is generally appreciated by antiquarians.

If you have a taste for angling, you can spend many profitable days at St. Avertin. The fishermen of Tours, with which it is connected by an electric tram, hold it in great esteem. But should you have no fondness for sport, an afternoon there will suffice to see everything, since it is rather poor in antiquities. Historically, however, it is an interesting place, especially to English people, who cannot fail to connect its name with that of a famous Englishman, Thomas à Becket. When exiled by Henry VIII, Becket, as we know, came to Tours; and in 1163 he was present at the council of prelates which Pope Alexander III had summoned there for the purpose of deposing the anti-Pope Victor. The archbishop was accompanied by his archdeacon, a Scotchman named Avertin. After the tragedy at Canterbury, Avertin

THE CHÂTEAU DE CANGÉ

decided to spend the remainder of his days in
solitude, and in order to effect his purpose
came to Touraine and hid himself in the
Cangé woods, near this village of the Cher.
The people of the village, then named St.
Pierre de Vençay, were so touched with his
virtue that they asked him to leave his retreat
and to live amongst them. He consented,
and until his death in 1180 carried out his
duties as a priest in their midst. Buried
in the parish church, he was henceforth
honoured as a saint, and the inhabitants, in
memory of him, changed the name of their
village to St. Avertin.

About a mile and a half from St. Avertin,
and half-way between that place and the
village of Larçay, we visited the Château de
Cangé. The road rises gently from the
village, with a screen of trees on the left
and the wooded hillside on the right. Near
the point where the Cher branches off into
the plain you come to the entrance to the
grounds of the château: an iron gateway and
a long carriage drive which leads up the hillside, through part of the woods where St.
Avertin lived, and brings you out at the top
in full view of the house. The prospect from
the terrace of this admirably situated château

is superb. In the distance is Tours, with its
dominant feature, the towers of the cathedral,
white and shining in the sun ; here and there
on the slope of the opposite side of the valley,
overlooking the Loire, are white châteaux and
country-houses ; and at the foot of the hill
on which you are standing winds the Cher,
mirroring the blue sky and the fleecy white
clouds of a perfect day.

The Château de Cangé, which is viewed
better from the back than the front, was built
at the end of the fifteenth or at the beginning
of the sixteenth century by one of the
members of the Conigham family,—probably
Pierre de Conigham. The founder of the
family was Jean de Conigham, Counsellor
and Chamberlain to Louis xi and Charles viii,
and a captain of the Scotch Guard. He came
to the district about the year 1489, bought
the Cangé estate from Jean de Saint Nectaire
and Jean de Montmorin, and died in 1495,
bequeathing his property to his son Pierre.
The Conighams were lords of Cangé until
1663, in which year the château and grounds
passed into other hands. Among the owners
in the eighteenth century was Pierre Imbert
de Chastres, who became Mayor of Tours,
but who is best known to fame as a collector

of manuscripts. His valuable collection of MSS. was sold to the King, and is now in the National Library, in Paris, classified under the name of the *Fonds Cangé*. The present owner is Comte de Pourtalès, who, by the bye, is Mayor of St. Avertin, by the inhabitants of which he is much esteemed, owing to the keen interest which he takes in everything concerning the prosperity of their village.

A short halt should be made at Larçay to see the remains of a Gallo-Roman *castellum*. Véretz, a little farther down the Cher, is worth a longer stay. It possesses a modern château built by Baron Paul de Richemont on the site of one which was constructed in 1519 by Jean de la Barre, chamberlain to Charles VIII, and which was almost entirely destroyed during the Revolution; but it is principally interesting on account of its Renaissance church and of the poet Paul Louis Courier, who lived on an estate called "La Chavonnière" not far away from the village. The "Vigneron de Véretz," as he was called, was murdered in the neighbouring forest of Larçay on April 10, 1825; and if you are a person of literary tastes you might pay a visit to the spot where he died. The place

is marked by a monument bearing an inscription. Another monument, with a medallion
portrait of this delicate poet, hellenist, and
pamphleteer, stands in the village of Véretz
itself.

CHAPTER XIV

UP THE CHER: AT STAINLESS CHENONCEAUX

UNLIKE so many other castles of Touraine, the Château of Chenonceaux, to which we came after a pleasant fifteen miles' run from Véretz, calls up only agreeable memories. Blois is stained with blood; Amboise was a prison; Loches, Chinon, Luynes, and a dozen more awaken thoughts of treason and the bad side of human nature. But Chenonceaux speaks to us of youth and love and poetry. The most charming figures of the fifteenth and sixteenth centuries—Diana of Poitiers, Mary Stuart, Gabrielle and Françoise de Mercœur—have occupied it and reflected their pretty faces in the waters of the Cher, on which it is built.

Chenonceaux is unique among the castles of France, for it is the only château which is built above a river and connected with each bank by a bridge. The idea was a

19   289

charming one, and could not have been conceived by a man alone. Thomas Bohier is
generally credited with having built it, but
I strongly suspect that his wife, Catherine
Briçonnet, who devoted the treasures which
her husband sent her from Italy to the building of this delightful residence, had more to
do with the initial idea than some historians
imagine. Bohier, who was a native of
Auvergne, was Count of Saint Ciergue,
général des finances for Normandy, and
lieutenant - general of the King's armies.
He followed Charles VIII during the Italian
campaign, and for a certain time was even
Viceroy of Naples. His taste for fine architecture and beautiful things in general is said
to have been acquired in Italy, and the date
at which he began to build Chenonceaux is
supposed to be 1515. The amount of money
he expended on his house was enormous, and,
judging by the motto which we find so many
times inscribed on doors, mantelpieces, and
walls—"S'il vient à point, m'en souviendra"
—he had little hope of ever seeing it completed. These words were, indeed, prophetic,
for he died at the Camp of Vigelli, in Italy,
on March 14, 1524, long before the finishing
touches had been put to it.

CHENONCEAUX FROM THE FRENCH GARDEN

You enter the château by a carved oak door (sixteenth century) on which are the words, "Devs spes mea salvs," and find yourself in a long vestibule ornamented with ancient pieces of carved furniture. This vestibule divides the château into two parts —one devoted to the needs of a modern house, the other preserved in the style of the sixteenth century. The latter portion, which is the only one presenting real interest, is entered by way of a room transformed into a dining-room. It is said to have been a guardroom originally, but it was more probably a waiting-room for the courtiers. Chenonceaux, although a royal residence, was less a palace than a country-house, and was not sufficiently large to have a guard-room. In addition to some fine specimens of Flemish tapestry, representing the Abduction of Helen, and a painted ceiling bearing Catherine de' Medici's initial, the room contains two beautiful wrought-iron candelabra, one on either side of the fireplace. The adjoining chapel, which is reached by a carved wood door of the sixteenth century to the left, is adorned with the arms of Thomas Bohier and those of his brother, Cardinal Bohier, and is well worth careful

inspection. The date, 1521, on these arms
and on the pretty tribune at the bottom
shows that the building was completed by
Thomas Bohier. The ogee ceiling and the
stained-glass windows show that the chapel
belongs to the architecture of the transitional
period which unites the Gothic era to that
of the Renaissance.

The waiting-room preceding this chapel
forms a centre from which the large apartments radiate. A door near the mantelpiece
leads to Catherine de' Medici's drawing-
room ; another, parallel to the door into
the chapel, opens into the apartments of
Louise de Vaudemont, a former owner of
Chenonceaux.

Catherine's *salon* is a superbly furnished
and decorated room. The mantelpiece is
attributed to Germain Pilon. Louise de
Vaudemont's apartments consist of three
rooms : bedroom, dressing-room, and library.
These were formerly hung in black, as
a sign of mourning for her husband,
Henry III, who, as a matter of fact, was
quite unworthy of her grief. The bedroom
has been transformed into a *salon*, and
furnished in the Francis I style. It is evident
from the furnishing of this and other rooms

CHENONCEAUX : THE VESTIBULE

THE DINING-ROOM AT CHENONCEAUX

on the ground-floor that those who have assisted in restoring Chenonceaux have wished to recall the three royal personages who successively owned the château — Francis, Catherine de' Medici, and Louise of Lorraine. As to the library, it is rather a dark little room. Over the door are the words, "Librairie de la royne Loyse." On one of the walls is a framed autograph letter of Henry IV, but the shelves contain few books such as one might expect to find in the library of a queen.

The first-floor of the castle is reached by a fine stone staircase branching off to the right of the vestibule. Let me here say that, up to the time of Francis I, staircases in houses and châteaux were invariably screw-shaped. If, as everything goes to show, the Chenonceaux staircase was built at the same time as those portions of the château which date from the days of Thomas Bohier, it was probably the first straight staircase in France. The vestibule on the first-floor contains some fine full-length portraits, and leads to the bedroom of Diana of Poitiers. The door through which you reach the room is low and narrow, and the interior decoration and furnishing are not so magnifi-

cent as one would have expected the bedroom
of a king's favourite to be. But it contains
some Flemish tapestries and a rather fine
mantelpiece; and I seem to remember
having seen there a portrait of the beautiful
duchess dressed as Diana the huntress.

Chenonceaux, by the bye, possesses some
really good pictures. I saw there a superb
canvas by Lesueur, representing three Muses,
a work by Vandyke, quite a number of
first-rate portraits by the great masters, and,
in the gallery on Diana's bridge (a gallery
with two storeys), a number of interesting
portraits of illustrious people of the sixteenth
century.

On retiring to Chenonceaux after the
assassination of Henry III, Louise of Lorraine
built some cells and a refectory on the upper
floor of this gallery for the Sisters of Mercy
whom the King of Spain sent to her.
These rooms are still to be seen. The
theatre in which Jean Jacques Rousseau
produced *L'Engagement Téméraire* and *Le
Devin du Village*, is at the end of the
gallery.

Before leaving the first-floor a visit should
be paid to the little terraces overlooking
the river. A splendid view of the stream

and the surrounding country through which it gracefully winds its way can be obtained from them. Then, by way of contrast, you should descend to the interior of the huge piles which support the main part of the building. Such is the size of these piles that, in addition to the prison and Catherine de' Medici's baths, it was found possible to build there a number of kitchens, a bakery, and a dining-room large enough to hold more than twenty servants.

As in the case of so many French châteaux, the architect who built Chenonceaux is unknown. It is to be presumed, however, that its plans were drawn up and put into execution by Frenchmen, and that it is the work of that school of Tours to which we owe Chambord and a large part of the Château of Blois.

After the death of Thomas Bohier and his wife, the Château of Chenonceaux came into the possession of Francis I. The King continued the work which they had left unfinished, but there is nothing to show that he took either much interest in it or visited it at all frequently. Only two visits are on record: one on August 24, 1546, when he felt the first symptoms of that

mysterious malady which killed him some
months later, and the other on April 14,
1545. There was a grand hunting-party
on the latter occasion, and among those
present were the heir to the throne and
Diana of Poitiers. It was probably at this
time that Diana conceived the idea of becoming the mistress of this splendid residence.
However that may be, the fact remains that
Francis had no sooner died than the new
King made over the château and its grounds
to her.

The next owner was Catherine de' Medici,
who, on becoming a widow in 1559, forced
Diana to exchange Chenonceaux for Chaumont. The château remained in her possession for thirty years, during which
time she made extensive alterations and
additions to it. Mary Stuart was a visitor
there, and the most elaborate fêtes were
given at the end of March 1559, as she
and her husband, Francis II, entered the
castle. The tenancy of Louise de Vaudemont
I have already mentioned. On her death
in 1601, she bequeathed the château to
her niece, Françoise of Lorraine, Duchesse
de Mercœur, the beautiful fiancée of César,
Duke of Vendôme. On the death of the

ANCIENT DOORWAY IN THE VESTIBULE AT
CHENONCEAUX

ANCIENT WELL AT CHENONCEAUX

last of the sons of César de Vendôme, Chenonceaux passed to his widow, Marie Anne of Bourbon, then to the Dowager Princess of Condé, and finally to the Duke of Bourbon, who bought the castle in 1720. He sold it in 1733 to Fermier Général Dupin. Madame Dupin entertained there in magnificent style, among her guests being Fontenelle, Buffon, Voltaire, Montesquieu, Mably, Marivaux, and Rousseau. Rousseau, who, in his youth, had been M. Dupin's secretary and his son's tutor, always spoke kindly of Chenonceaux. It is in his *Confessions*, I believe, that you will find his remark that " Les Français sont en Touraine, non à Paris " ; and elsewhere he exclaims :

"Que je me plais sous ces ombrages !
Que j'aime ces flots argentés !"

Madame Dupin passed the worst days of the Revolution at Chenonceaux. The buildings were spared by the revolutionaries, but they compelled her to burn her securities and a valuable collection of pictures and portraits, collected during three centuries, in front of a tree of Liberty. She died at Chenonceaux in 1799, at the age of ninety-three, bequeathing the château to her nephew, M. de Villeneuve. It next came into the possession of his only son, Count René de Villeneuve, who began its restoration. George Sand, the Count's cousin-german, was a frequent visitor to Chenonceaux during his ownership. In 1864 the château was sold to the chemist, Pelouze. It is now owned by M. Terry, a wealthy Cuban gentleman, to whose family is due the credit of having undertaken the complete restoration of the château. Up to the present more than two million francs have been expended on the house and gardens, and work was still in progress when we visited his beautiful European home.

Such, in brief, is the history of stainless Chenonceaux. It has had the rare good fortune to be undisturbed by violent events, and let us hope that it will never know the worst side of history.

CHAPTER XV

IN THE SARTHE: FROM LE LUDE TO JARZÉ

ALMOST imperceptibly the summer had slipped away. September had come, and with it autumn's messengers. In the early morning, before the sun had had time to warm the air, the cobwebbed furze-bushes at the sides of the lanes of Touraine were covered with myriads of tiny dewdrops, whose sparkle strangely mimicked the hoar-frost of winter. The long rows of poplars, which were rapidly changing their green foliage for one that was yellow and scanty, faded into a misty distance. On low lying meadows near the Loire and the Cher the ground was purple with thousands upon thousands of colchicum blossoms,—the " naked ladies " of our English fields, and so called in rustic language because of the meadow saffron's entire lack of leaves, which do not grow until the spring, its graceful pose, and

its tender tint of mauve suffused with a rosy
blush. As to the grapes, these were rapidly
reddening on the vines, and in a few weeks'
time would be gathered in amidst laughter
and song.

On the recommendation of Balzac, who
writes with his usual enthusiasm on the
subject of the vintage and autumns of Touraine,
we were much tempted to linger on in the
ancient province. But the call of the city,
which we had succeeded in entirely forgetting
for more than three months, was, unfortunately, imperative, and our departure thence
was now a question merely of days. Besides,
the main purpose for which we had come to
this part of France had been accomplished;
and I can assure you we prided ourselves not
a little on the fact that there was not a
château or a ruined castle of importance which
we had not visited. "I see that you have
seen everything," said some one to whom I had
enumerated the places at which we had called;
"that is, everything in Touraine. But what
about the châteaux of the Sarthe? Geogra-
phically, they are out of the district you
proposed to explore. But, now that you are
here and within such a short distance of them,
you must not think of neglecting the principal

LE LUDE: FAÇADE FACING THE PARK

THE FRENCH GARDEN AT LE LUDE

one amongst them—Le Lude. Palustre, you know, says that it would be difficult to find a more elegant example of the architecture of the early days of the Renaissance than this beautiful château." As this suggested excursion would add, we were told, but two more days at the most to the length of our stay, we decided to undertake it. Tours, therefore, saw us once more. We made a quick run from that town to Château la Vallière, which is noted for its picturesque lake and forest, and thence to Le Lude, an old and prosperous little town on the Loire. The scenery we encountered on the way consisted largely of woodland. In fact, the whole of the Sarthe has the aspect of an extensive forest, the department gaining this appearance owing to the numerous hedges which separate the fields, and the clumps of tall trees which are dotted here and there.

Our adviser was certainly right in recommending us not to miss the Château of Le Lude. Its stateliness, the beauty of its ornamentation on pilasters and dormer-windows, and the charm of its gardens place it on an equal footing with some of the most important of the châteaux of the Loire. The gardens, which are even finer than those at

Chenonceaux, are especially noteworthy. The garden *à l'anglaise* is situated on a raised terrace overlooking the Loir and facing the southern façade of the château, and is embellished along its entire length of two hundred yards with superb marble vases, which I believe are Italian work of the sixteenth century. At the end of the terrace is also a fine marble group, representing Hercules and Antæus, by Mongendre, a Mans sculptor who lived about the end of the reign of Louis xiv. Beneath, and bordering the Loir, is the French garden, set out in that formal manner which accords so well with the lines of the eastern or eighteenth century façade of the château facing the river.

The interior of the château, in spite of the richness of its decoration, proved a disappointment in comparison with what we had seen outside. The four huge machicolated towers give the idea that the building is a very roomy one, but on entering you find that this is not so. With the exception of the large and small drawing-rooms, and the Salle des Fêtes, the rooms are small and, withal, astonishingly dark. The electric light had to be turned on even in the fairly large Salle des Fêtes in order to be able to see the sculptured mantel-

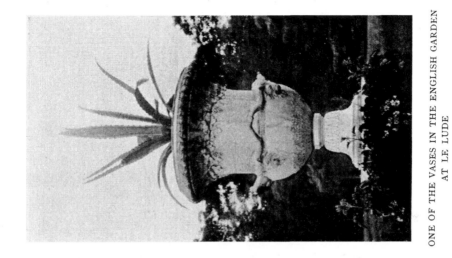

AN ANCIENT SUNDIAL IN THE GROUNDS OF
LE LUDE

ONE OF THE VASES IN THE ENGLISH GARDEN
AT LE LUDE

THE CHÂTEAU DES CARMES AT LA FLÈCHE

piece to advantage ! Yet the sun outside was
shining magnificently from a cloudless sky.
This sombreness is caused, of course, by the
immense thickness of the walls and the equally
unavoidable narrowness of the windows, and
is one of the disadvantages, from the modern
point of view, of most of these ancient
châteaux. Otherwise, the apartments are
above criticism. On all sides in the dining-
room, library, and drawing-rooms are choice
furniture, pictures, tapestries, and other works
of art ; a little oratory in one of the towers is
decorated with remarkable mural paintings by
artists of the school of Rosso and Primatice ;
the recently completed carved stone staircase
is a fine example of modern work ; and the
bedrooms, in one of which Henry IV slept
during his visit to Le Lude in 1598, as shown
by a framed letter preserved there, are interesting either for their contents or their
historical associations.

The Château of Le Lude, which forms
a large quadrilateral, surrounding a rather
diminutive courtyard, was built by members
of the Daillon family. Jacques de Daillon
began to build it on the site of a feudal castle
about the year 1520 ; the work was continued
by his widow, on behalf of their son Jean,

and it was completed by Guy de Daillon, the son of Jean. Later owners made additions or alterations. Thus, Thimoléon de Daillon, whose sundial, bearing the arms of his family and those of his wife, with their initials and the date 1649, stands in the garden facing the eighteenth century façade, directed his attention principally to the gardens; whilst the Marquis de la Vieuville, who restored the mansion at a cost of over £11,000, pulled down the western wing which connected the two towers nearest the town, replaced it by the present buildings and three-arched portico, and built the eastern façade. The restoration of Le Lude was continued in 1853 by the present owner, the Marquis de Talhouët, and has only recently been completed. The northern façade, with its equestrian statue of Jacques de Daillon, and the monumental entrance to the grounds from the town form part of the work he has had carried out.

It was inevitable that, having come so far as Le Lude, we should proceed a little farther towards Jarzé, which held forth the prospect of an interesting château, since we were informed it had been built by Jean Bourré, the builder of Langeais. On our way there we

THE CHÂTEAU DE BAUGÉ

THE CHÂTEAU DE JARZÉ

came first to La Flèche and then to Baugé, both famous places. The former is celebrated for its military school, which, founded by Napoleon in 1808, in ecclesiastical buildings dating from about the middle of the seventeenth century, has produced many of France's finest soldiers. But this Prytanée interested us less than the pretty Château des Carmes, a former convent near the bridge that crosses the Loir. There is also a château at Baugé, — a picturesque, weather-beaten building of the fifteenth century which is attributed to King René, who, according to legend, was very fond of this town and district. The former residence of the good King of Naples (he was surnamed " Le Bon " on account of his paternal character, his pacific government, his constant serenity under ill fortune, and his love for art and literature) is now the Mairie and Gendarmery. Its best preserved portions are the sculptured doorway to the tower facing the Place du Château and the winding staircase within, a staircase surmounted by a fan-vaulting on which are armorial bearings supposed to be those of King René. Whilst on the road from Baugé to Jarzé you get a view, on the left, of the towers of the Château de Landifer,

20

which should be visited if you wish to be able to say that you have explored the Sarthe thoroughly. Not professing to have set out to do that, we did not find the time to see this partly Renaissance, partly modern castle.

Jarzé is a plain, a very plain country-house situated on an eminence, whence an extensive view can be obtained of much of the surrounding country, even as far as Angers, twenty-seven miles away, when the weather is good. Having Langeais in our mind's eye, we expected to find something a good deal more castle-like than this. But it appeared we had paid our visit a little more than one hundred and ten years too late, for nearly the whole of the castle built by Jean Bourré in 1500 was burnt down in 1794. Two paintings over the doors in the Petit Salon of its comparatively modern successor show its outward appearance. The still remaining portions of the old castle consist of a small guardroom and a little oratory with vaulted ceiling on which are paintings of cupids. The other rooms are frankly modern. Yet they have one peculiarity which is certainly worthy of being mentioned, *i.e.* that what beauties they may possess lie hidden beneath their lath and plaster ceilings. Beneath these, in all probability, are others with painted beams. One of the sons of the owner, M. Cloquemin, took us into a bedroom where the ceiling had been pierced, and through the hole, sure enough, we could see the original plafond, with its ornamentation almost as fresh as the day it was painted. The restoration of Jarzé might, therefore, be worth undertaking.

With the Château of Jarzé we brought our sight-seeing to an end. Even our motor-car seemed to realise that we had visited enough châteaux, for, on returning to La Flèche, there occurred the only serious breakdown we had had during the three months we spent in central France. The next day, however, we were once more on the road, and on reaching Tours we took the train for Paris. The beautiful Loire, seen now and then from our carriage window, flashed in the sunlight and set up recollections of the happy days we had spent upon its banks. Royal Amboise came into sight and faded away; the stout towers of Chaumont rose once more from the trees on its wooded ridge and likewise disappeared; and the northern wing of the Castle of Blois towered for an instant above the gray little town which had been our starting-place. That last glimpse of the work of the Renaissance made us perceive more clearly than anything else had done that our summer sojourn was over.

INDEX